S0-BHZ-378

DRAMATIC

MISCELLANIES.

VOL. II.

AMS PRESS
NEW YORK

DRAMATIC MICELLANIES:

CONSISTING OF

CRITICAL OBSERVATIONS

ON SEVERAL

PLAYS OF SHAKSPEARE:

WITH

A REVIEW OF HIS PRINCIPAL CHARACTERS, AND THOSE OF VARIOUS EMINENT WRITERS,

AS REPRESENTED

BY MR. GARRICK, AND OTHER CELEBRATED COMEDIANS.

WITH ANECDOTES OF DRAMATIC POETS, ACTORS, &c.

BY THOMAS DAVIES,

AUTHOR of MEMOIRS of the LIFE of DAVID GARRICK, ESQ.

IN THREE VOLUMES.

VOL. II.

LONDON:

Printed for the AUTHOR, and ſold at his Shop, in GREAT RUSSELL-STREET, COVENT-GARDEN.

M.DCC.LXXXIII.

Library of Congress Cataloging in Publication Data

Davies, Thomas, 1712?-1785.
Dramatic micellanies [sic] consisting of critical observations on several plays of Shakespeare.

1. Shakespeare, William, 1564-1616--Stage history.
2. Shakespeare, William, 1564-1616--Criticism and interpretation. 3. Theater--England--History.
I. Title.
PR3095.D3 1973 822.3'3 75-163675
ISBN 0-404-01991-9 (v. 1)

Reprinted from an original in the collections of The Newark Public Library

From the edition of 1783, London
First AMS edition published in 1973
Manufactured in the United States of America

International Standard Book Number:
Complete Set: 0-404-01990-0
Volume Two: 0-404-01992-7

AMS PRESS INC.
NEW YORK, N.Y. 10003

DRAMATIC

MISCELLANIES.

All's well that ends well.

CHAPTER XXI.

Unpromising fable to All's well that ends well.—*Shakspeare's creative power.*—*Revival of this comedy in* 1741.—*Sickness of Milward.*—*Mrs. Woffington.*—*Death of Milward.*—*His character.*—*Superstition of the actors.*—*Parolles.*—*Macklin and The. Cibber.*—*Chapman and Berry commended.*—All's well that ends well *revived by Garrick.*—*Distribution of the parts.*—*Abuse of wardship.*—*Fascinating power of certain worthless characters.*—*Lully, Swift, and Lord Rivers.*—*Word* Christendom.

dom. — *Helen's deſcription of Parolles.* — *Definition of* clown, *or* fool.—*His occupation.*— *Deſcription from Johnſon and Steevens.* — *B. Jonſon and Fletcher.* — *Shakſpeare's ſuperior knowledge of nature and the qualities of his auditors.* — *Jonſon not averſe to mirth in tragedy.* — *His Sejanus and Catiline.* — *Condition of phyſicians in England, France, and Germany.*— *Helen's delicacy.*

A Phyſician's daughter curing a king, diſtempered with a fiſtula, by a recipe of her dead father, is the hiſtory on which this play is founded; a plot ſtrange and unpromiſing. But the genius of Shakſpeare meets with no obſtacle from the uncouthneſs of the materials he works upon. Action and character are the chief engines he employs in this comedy, and he raiſes abundance of mirth from the ſituations in which they are placed. Parolles and Lafeu are admirable contraſts, from the colliſion of of whofe humours perpetual laughter is produced.

Helen's fcheme, of gaining her hufband's affections by paffing on him for a miftrefs, has been adopted with fuccefs by other dramatifts; particularly by Shirley in the Gamefter, and Cibber in his firft comedy of Love's laft Shift.

All's well that ends well, after having lain more than a hundred years undifturbed upon the prompter's fhelf, was, in October, 1741, revived at the theatre in Drury-lane. Milward, who acted the King, is faid to have caught a diftemper which proved fatal to him, by wearing, in this part, a too light and airy fuit of clothes, which he put on after his fuppofed recovery. He felt himfelf feized with a fhivering; and was afked, by one of the players, how he found himfelf? 'How is it poffible for me,' he faid, with fome pleafantry, 'to be fick, when I have fuch a phyfician as Mrs. Woffington?' This elegant and beautiful actrefs was the Helen of the play.

His diſtemper, however, increaſed, and ſoon after hurried him to his grave.

So pleaſing an actor as Milward deſerves more than a ſlight remembrance. In the Memoirs of Garrick's Life, I ſpoke of him as one who was not without a great ſhare of merit, but was too apt to indulge himſelf in ſuch an extenſion of voice as approached to vociferation. He prided himſelf ſo much in the harmony and ſweetneſs of his tones, that he was heard to ſay, in a kind of rapture, after throwing out ſome paſſionate ſpeeches in a favourite part, that he wiſhed *he could ſalute the ſweet echo*, meaning his voice. His Luſignan, in Zara, was not much inferior to Mr. Garrick's repreſentation of that part. —— Milward choſe Booth for his model; and, notwithſtanding his inferiority to that accompliſhed tragedian, he was the only performer in tragedy, who, if he had ſurvived, could have approached to our great Roſcius; who, though he would always have been the firſt, yet, in that caſe, would not have

have been the only, actor in tragedy. Milward died about a fortnight after Garrick's first appearance on the stage.

The part of Parolles was, by Fleetwood, the manager, promised to Macklin; but Theophilus Cibber, by some sort of artifice, as common in theatres as in courts, snatched it from him, to his great displeasure. Berry was the Lafeu, and Chapman the Clown and Interpreter. All's well that ends well was termed, by the players, the unfortunate comedy, from the disagreeable accidents which fell out several times during the acting of it. Mrs. Woffington was suddenly taken with illness as she came off the stage from a scene of importance. Mrs. Ridout, a pretty woman and a pleasing actress, after having played Diana one night, was, by the advice of her physician, forbidden to act during a month. Mrs. Butler, in the Countess of Rousillon, was likewise seized with a distemper in the progress of this play.

All's

All's well that ends well, however, had ſuch a degree of merit, and gave ſo much general ſatisfaction to the public, that, in ſpite of the ſuperſtition of ſome of the players, who wiſhed and entreated that it might be diſcontinued, upon Mr. Delane's undertaking to act the King after Milward's deceaſe, it was again brought forward and applauded.

Cibber's Parolles, notwithſtanding his grimace and falſe ſpirit, met with encouragement. This actor, though his vivacity was mixed with too much pertneſs, never offended by flatneſs and inſipidity. Chapman was admirable in the clowns of Shakſpeare. Berry's Lafeu was the true portrait of a choleric old man and a humouriſt. Milward was, in the King, affecting; and Delane, in the ſame part, reſpectable.

Under the direction of Mr. Garrick, in 1757, All's well that ends well was again revived. Mrs. Pritchard acted the Counteſs; Miſs Macklin, Helen; Mrs. Davies, Diana;

Diana. Parolles, Woodward; Lafeu, Berry; and Davies, the King. With the help of a pantomime, it was acted ſeveral nights.

Act I. Scene I.

BERTRAM.

I muſt attend his majeſty's command,
To whom I am *in ward.*

No prerogative of the crown, in the time of the feudal ſyſtem, was eſteemed more honourable, or was indeed more profitable, than that of *wardſhip*; nor was any part of kingly power more ſubject to fraudulent abuſe, to tyranny and oppreſſion. So cruelly had King John, and ſome of his predeceſſors, exerted an undue influence over their wards, that the fourth, fifth, ſixth, ſeventh, forty-third, and forty-fourth, articles of the great charter, are all expreſſly written with an intention to reſtrain the power of the crown within proper limits reſpecting wardſhips.

Helen,

Helen, after reflecting on Bertram, the object of her love, who had immediately before taken his leave to ſet out for the court, on ſeeing Parolles, by her obſervations on him, prepares the reader for ſome notable entertainment which is to enſue. Her tenderneſs in diſcuſſing of his vices is a ſtrong, though delicate, confeſſion of her love to Bertram;

HELEN.

——— I love him for his ſake;
And yet I know him a notorious liar,
Think him a great way fool, ſolely a coward:
Yet theſe fix'd evils ſit ſo fit on him,
That they take place when virtue's ſteely brows
Look bleak to the cold wind.

There is ſuch a relative charm, in that which in any manner appertains to the perſon we love, let it be never ſo inſignificant and worthleſs, that we are ſure to be pleaſed with it, becauſe it calls to mind the object of our affections. Helen's remark, that the ſlight and worthleſs, provided they have talents to excite gaiety and cheerfulneſs,

cheerfulneſs, are often preferred to the meritorious, but leſs pliable in temper, is equally juſt; and of this many inſtances can be produced.

Lully, the famous French muſician, was a debauched fellow and a voluptuary; his company was notwithſtanding the delight of all parties, of the witty and the gay, the grave and the learned. He excelled in mimicry and the art of inventing and telling little ſtories. He was not over nice in the ſelection of his terms, but indulged a licentious humour to the height. The ſevere Boileau, who was not ſo much ſought after and invited as Lully, wondered at the diſtinction beſtowed upon that obſcene buffoon, as he called him; and would often chide Moliere for his taſte in admiring his talent of exciting mirth, for Moliere was as ſilent in Lully's company as Garrick uſed to be in Foote's. He was always inviting him to indulge his talent: 'Lully, *fais nous rire*,' 'Make us laugh,' was the conſtant addreſs of the great dramatic

matic writer to the merry muſician. But this happy talent of pleaſing, in a man of merit, and not abſolutely abandoned, may be reconciled to conveniency, if not approved by reaſon. But Parolles was marked with ſo many vices, that we can hardly juſtify the countenance given him by his ſuperiors. But there is, in ſome men, an uncommon power of ſubduing the minds of others, ſo that, in ſpite of a thouſand reaſons againſt it, you are ſo bewitched as not to diſcern their vices, though ever ſo groſs, through the inchanted veil which they throw over them.

Dr. Swift was, of all men, if we may believe himſelf, the moſt cautious in the ſelection of his friends and companions. Earl Rivers, the father of the unfortunate Savage, was, in Swift's opinion, the moſt profligate and abandoned of men: and yet he was ſo inchanted by his irreſiſtible power of pleaſing in converſation,* that he could

* Amongſt other allurements, Homer gives Juno, to charm Jupiter, is the attraction of perſuaſive converſation.

Παρφασις, η τ' εκλεψε νοον ϖυκα ϖερ φρονεοντων.

ILIAD. Lib. XIV.

could not help declaring, that 'he loved the dog dearly.'

The ſame ſcene continued.

HELEN.

——— With a world
Of fond adoptious *Chriſtendoms.*

The word *Chriſtendom* is no where uſed in this ſenſe by Shakſpeare, I believe, except by Prince Arthur, in King John, act iv. ſcene 1:

——— By my *Chriſtendom,*
So I were out of priſon, and kept ſheep,
I ſhould be as merry as the day is long.

Swearing by *Chriſtendom* is ſwearing by all that is dear.

HELEN.

But the compoſition, that your valour and fear make in you, is the virtue of a good *wing.* I like it well.

Dr. Warburton produces abundance of argument to ſupport his emendations of the text. He would ſubſtitute *ming* for *wing*, a word common, he ſays, in Shakſpeare and the writers of the age: —— but where, pray? Dr. Johnſon rejects his *ming*,

ming, but cannot preſerve the original word, *wing*, without allowing it to be a metaphor taken from hawking; and this Mr. Steevens, I think, very ſubſtantially proves. Helen's meaning, then, may be thus plainly deduced: "The agreement, which is ſettled between your valour, which is paſſive, and your fear, which is active, will carry you through all dangers; and you will ſoar, with a well-poiſed *wing*, very ſafely."

HELEN.

The mightieſt ſpace in fortune nature brings
To join like likes, and kiſs like native things.
Impoſſible be ſtrange attempts to thoſe
That weigh their pain with ſenſe, and do ſuppoſe
What hath been cannot be.

I agree with Dr. Johnſon, that theſe lines are not without obſcurity; but our great poet's conceptions were ſo quick, that he very often did not allow himſelf time to give them proper clothing. In this paſſage, Shakſpeare gives only the feelings of the character. "There is

(ſays

(ſays Helen) a certain power in nature to ſhorten or contract the greateſt poſſible diſtance that fortune can make between two perſons. Let thoſe talk of impoſſibilities who ſcrupulouſly weigh every difficulty from their own cowardly ſenſations: they do not conſider, that what has once happened may again fall out.

Act. I. Scene III.

Counteſs, Steward, and Clown.

The character of the Fool, or Clown, was originally introduced into the world to ſupply the want of that freedom in converſation which was unknown to the ſavage manners of our anceſtors. When half the kingdom was in a ſtate of ſlavery, under the elder Plantagenets of the Norman race, and their immediate ſucceſſors; when vaſſalage univerſally prevailed, and Engliſhmen were ſubject to the will of a deſpotic king and his haughty and imperious barons; the trade of war was the

 principal

principal commerce of all the nations in Europe, and tilts and tournaments their great, and almoſt ſole, amuſement. The ſocial intercourſe, and elegant diverſions, which ſo happily employ both ſexes in this refined age, were then utterly unknown; inſtead of the entertainments of the ſtage, which we now enjoy in its almoſt perfect ſtate, the myſteries and moralities, of which ſome ſpecimens are preſerved in old writers, were the only theatrical ſpectacles exhibited from Richard the Second's days to the reign of Queen Elizabeth. Myſtery was the tragedy, and morality the comedy: the latter, perhaps, owed its origin to the clown, or fool, in a motley dreſs, which every noble family in the kingdom entertained as a neceſſary appendage of ſtate and grandeur. Nature will inſiſt upon her rights in ſome ſhape or other; and mirth is ſo congenial to man, that it muſt have a vent. A ſarcaſtic, or perhaps a harmleſs, jeſt, from one equal to another, in the rough days of the feudal ſyſtem, would, in

all

all likelihood, have brought about ſerious conſequences, and perhaps ended in a ſingle combat. But kings could not live in their palaces, nor great barons in their caſtles, without ſome inſtrument to excite merriment. They had no wits, indeed, to flatter them; but they had, what men of the moſt refined underſtanding love better, a fool to laugh at.

A fellow, dreſſed in a patched coat, guarded with yellow, was hired, at a certain ſalary, to divert the great man and his gueſts. All now was ſafe; for nobody could pretend to be angry with the ſarcaſtic gibes or ſaucy petulancies of a party-coloured hireling; one too, who was himſelf the butt of the company. The fool treated all alike; the maſter and his gueſts were equally the objects of his ſatirical mirth; and I make no doubt that a keen-witted fellow would ſometimes revenge the diſgrace of ſituation on his betters, by uttering ſevere reproach and home truth under the cover of a joke, which no man durſt reſent without being expoſed to the deriſion of the company.

Viola, in Twelfth Night, aptly deſcribes the buſineſs of a fool by profeſſion:

This fellow is wiſe enough to play the fool,
And to do that well craves a kind of wit.
He muſt obſerve their mood on whom he jeſts,
The quality of the perſons, and the time;
And, like the haggard, check at every feather
That comes before his eye.———

Riccoboni, in his hiſtory of the Italian theatre, deduces the Harlequin and Scapin from the Roman Sannio: "For the Sannio is nothing elſe, he ſays, but our buffoon." To ſupport his hypotheſis, he alledges the authority of Cicero, in his book De Oratore: '*Quid enim poteſt tam ridiculum quam Sannio eſſe? Qui ore, vultu, imitandis motibus, voce, denique corpore, ridetur ipſo.*'

Barrett, in his Alvearie, ſeems to be of the ſame opinion with reſpect to the Sannio, or fool, as Riccoboni, "*The vice, or geſtor, began the dance.—Sannio ſaltationem occepit.*"

None

None of our old dramatic writers have made ſuch frequent and happy uſe of this character as Shakſpeare. The immediate predeceſſor of his clown he found in The Moralities, which never were without a fellow dreſſed in a long coat, a cap on his head with a pair of aſſes ears, and a dagger of lath* by his ſide. The ſport between him and his adverſary, the devil, was a perpetual ſource of mirth and loud laughter.

Ben Jonſon, and his friends Beaumont and Fletcher, very ſeldom employed this merry agent in their plays. Their claſſical learning placed them, it is thought, above the uſe of ſo mean an inſtrument. It may be ſo: but, I believe, their pieces did not ſucceed the better for their contempt of the public taſte. The ſtage was then in its infancy, nor could the people, all at once, be weaned from their baubles, their caps and bells, and party-coloured liveries.

* Johnſon and Steevens's Shakſpeare.

Shakſpeare, who underſtood human nature better than Jonſon and his admirers, was reſolved not to reſign an engine of which he could make ſo notable an uſe. He had taken full meaſure of the underſtanding, humour, and taſte, of his audience; and no phyſician was ever more accurately acquainted with the pulſe of his patient than our poet was with the peculiar diet which would pleaſe the palates of the good folks in this metropolis. After a ſerious, or pathetic, ſcene, he knew that his clown would revive the mirth, cheer the ſpirits, and dry the tears, of his auditors. And, I know not, after all, if the man, who can excite our mirth, and command our grief, ſucceſſively, may not be the beſt dramatic cook to prepare entertainment for a people ſo melancholy and ſo merry, ſo ſprightly and ſo ſad, as the Engliſh are generally ſaid to be.

So convinced was Shakſpeare that his countrymen could not be ſatisfied with their dramatic exhibitions without ſome

mixture

mixture of merriment, that, in his moſt ſerious plays, he has thrown in characters of levity, or oddity, to enliven the ſcene. In King John we have the baſtard Falconbridge; in Macbeth the witches; who, though not abſolutely comic, never fail to provoke laughter. In Julius Cæſar, Caſca and the mob; in Hamlet, Polonius, the grave-diggers, and Oſtrick; nay, in Othello, his laſt and moſt finiſhed tragedy, beſides a happily-conceived drunken ſcene of Caſſio, we are preſented with the follies of a Roderigo: theſe comic characters, placed in proper ſituations to produce action ariſing from the plot, never failed to raiſe gaiety and diverſion amidſt ſcenes of the moſt affecting pathos and the moſt afflicting terror. What affords the moſt evident proofs of our author's infallible judgement and ſagacity is, that, notwithſtanding the great alteration and improvement in the public taſte, reſpecting the amuſements of the theatre, theſe characters and ſcenes never fail to produce the ſame effect at this day; and who, after all, is offended with the idle politics and ſilly pedantry of Polonius, after admiring the wonderful interview of Hamlet and the ghoſt? Who does not laugh at the prattling and goſſipries of the nurſe, when Juliet has taken a ſad and mournful leave of her beloved Romeo?

Ben Jonſon was not averſe to the uſe of the characters and language of comedy in his tragedies; but Ben underſtood not the art of blending them ſo happily as not to deſtroy the effect of either. In his Sejanus, he introduces a ſcene between the principal character of the play and Eudemus the phyſician. Sejanus gravely interrogates the doctor concerning the effect of the phyſic he adminiſters to the ladies, his patients, and is anxious to know which of them, during the operation, made the moſt wry faces: this is below farce.—Nay, ſo loſt is this learned author to all ſenſe of decency and decorum, that Catiline, in the grand ſcene of conſpirators, in Act

III.

III. threatens one of his young aſſociates with the ſevereſt puniſhment for his reluctance to ſubmit to the moſt infamous of all crimes!

The ſcene continued.

CLOWN.

I ſhall never have the bleſſing of God till I have iſſue of my body; for, they ſay, bearns are bleſſings.

The clown's opinion correſponds with that of all mankind, and more particularly with the Jews. They hold barrenneſs to be a great curſe. No people in the world multiply ſo faſt as they. Sir James Porter, in his letters on the Turkiſh nation, after informing us that, by a certain law in the Alcoran, when no heirs male are left in the family the eſtate is immediately forfeited to the emperor, aſſures his readers it is next to a miracle to hear of the effects of a Jewiſh family being forfeited to the Sultan for want of heirs.

COUNTESS.

The myſtery of your *lonelineſs*——

Which,

Which, I think, a happy emendation of Theobald from *lovelineſs*.

Mr. Tyrrwhit prefers, inſtead of *loneli-neſs*, a ſuggeſtion of Mr. Hall in favour of *lowlineſs*; but Mr. Steevens ſeems to underſtand the language of love better than his friend, and juſtifies Theobald. If Mr. Tyrrwhit wants an authority for a perſon in love being fond of retirement and ſoli-tude, Romeo and Juliet will give him one. Romeo, Act I.

MONTAGUE.

Away from light ſteals home my giddy ſon,
And private in the chamber pens himſelf.

And Roſalind, in As you like it, when ſhe can no longer enjoy the company of Or-lando, leaves her couſin Cælia to find a ſhadow and to ſleep.

HELEN.

My friends were poor, but honeſt; ſo is my love!

Helen pleads that, although ſhe is no higher in rank than a phyſician's daughter, yet her love is as much mark'd for ſincerity

as

as her relations were eſteemed for their integrity.

In no part of Europe is the worth of a learned and ſkilful phyſician ſo well underſtood, and ſo generouſly rewarded, as in England. In France, till very lately, phyſicians were placed in a lower claſs. The ancients, in the opinion of Dr. Middleton, who wrote a Treatiſe *de Conditione Medicorum apud Antiquos*, rated them not much higher than ſlaves. In Flanders, the cuſtomary fee, to a phyſician, is no more than half a crown: I believe it is the ſame through Holland and all Germany.

But Helen's love is as honeſt as her parentage. It appears, throughout the whole play, that the paſſion of this ſweet girl is of the nobleſt kind: 'Nature, ſays Shakſpeare in Hamlet, is fine in love;' that is, it purifies and refines our paſſions. Before marriage Helen diminiſhes the blemiſhes of Parolles, becauſe he is the conſtant companion of Bertram, and after marriage,

marriage, though ſhe might reaſonably exclaim againſt the ſeducer of her huſband, with the utmoſt delicacy ſhe reſtrains herſelf from the leaſt reproach; nay, converts a queſtion, implying cenſure, to a mark of honour.

CHAPTER XXII.

Meaning of Good faith acroſs. — *Helen's tax of impudence, &c. — Theobald defended. — Several paſſages explained. — A ſcene of Parolles.—His character.—Compared with that of Beſſus.— King and no King intended to have been revived by Mr. Garrick. — Why thrown aſide.—Inceſt an improper ſubject for a play.— Don Sebaſtian.—Maſſinger's unnatural combat.—Beſſus a pander as well as a coward. — Cowardice in the abſtract.—No proper ſubject of mirth. --- Parolles admirable to the laſt.---Time and Dr. Johnſon.---Helen's ring.---Queen Elizabeth and the Earl of Eſſex.*

Act. II. Scene I. King and Lafeu.

LAFEU.

Pardon, my lord, for me and for my tidings.

KING.

I'll ſee thee to ſtand up.

LAFEU.

LAFEU.

——— Then here's a man
Stands that has bought his pardon. I would you
Had kneel'd, my lord, to aſk me mercy; and
That at my bidding you could ſo ſtand up.

KING.

I would I had, ſo I had broke thy pate,
And aſk'd thee mercy for it.

LAFEU.

——— *Good faith, acroſs.*

IT was neceſſary to quote theſe ſeveral ſpeeches that the ſenſe of the laſt words might be better underſtood. Dr. Johnſon interprets the expreſſion, 'a croſs,' to mean, a paſs in wit that miſcarries. I think quite otherwiſe. The King, not being, through infirmity, able to raiſe Lafeu from kneeling, ſays he will 'ſee him to ſtand up.' Lafeu wiſhes that the King, even on the humiliating condition of aſking pardon of him, his ſubject, could ſtand as firmly. 'So would I,' replied the King, 'though I had broken your pate at the

the ſame time, and aſked your pardon for it.' The anſwer, of 'Good faith, acroſs,' is as much as to ſay, 'With all my heart, ſir, though you had broken my head acroſs;' which, in the language of thoſe days, ſignified a very ſevere blow or contuſion on the head. Twefth Night, act v. ſcene 5. Sir Andrew Aguecheek. '*He has broke my head acroſs*, and given Sir Toby a bloody coxcomb too.'

KING.

Thus he his ſpecial nothing ever prologues.

So, in the Merchant of Venice, Antonio characteriſes Gratiano:

Gratiano ſpeaks an infinite deal of nothing.

KING.

Upon thy certainty and confidence
What dar'ſt thou venture?

HELEN.

——— Tax of impudence,
A ſtrumpet's boldneſs, a divulged ſhame,
Traduc'd by odious ballads; my maiden's name

Sear'd

Sear'd otherwife ; no worfe of worft extended,
With vileft tortures let my life be ended.

Mr. Steevens, in his very ingenious note upon this obfcure paffage, has not, I think, cleared all the difficulties of it.—— He imagines that Helen, in her covenant with the King, to fuffer all manner of indignities if fhe does not perform the promifed cure, excepts the violation of her chaftity. But fhe is fo confident of fuccefs, that fhe does not imagine a poffibility of failure ; befides, the infamous violation of a virgin, or woman, has been no part of the penal laws in Chriftian Europe, though it certainly was the practice in old Rome, and efpecially during the emperors. If we attend a little to the mode of expreffion, we may fairly conclude, that Helen, by ' no worfe of worft extended,' meant, that the branding her maiden character with the name of a whore was the worft punifhment that could be extended to her.

Scene

Scene the third,

LAFEU.

We make trifles of terrors, enſconcing ourſelves into ſeeming knowledge, when we ſhould ſubmit ourſelves to an unknown fear.

Our author, in ſeveral of his plays, ridicules the philoſophers of the times in which he lived, who endeavoured to account for all uncommon appearances in nature, either by attributing them to the agency of ſecond cauſes, or to ſome principle ſtill more bold and uncertain: whereas Shakſpeare inſinuates, that it would be more modeſt to confeſs our ignorance, in things beyond our capacities to comprehend, and attribute their exiſtence to ſome cauſe unknown to us.

KING.

——— Good alone
Is good without a name. Vileneſs is ſo.

That is, 'if vice be deteſtable, as it certainly is, from its intrinſic baſeneſs; ſo muſt virtue be, from its own purity, without the help of any addition whatſoe-ever.'

I believe Mr. Steevens, whom nothing eſcapes, is rather beforehand with me in this explanation, or at leaſt in ſomething very near it.

KING.

My honour's at the ſtake; which to *defeat*,
I muſt produce my power.

Mr. Theobald, who was not well pleaſed with his exaltation to the throne of dulneſs, embraces every opportunity to turn into ridicule Pope's emendations of Shakſpeare; he laughs at the word *defeat*, and terms it nonſenſical; he propoſes to ſubſtitute the word *defend* in its room. Dr. Farmer candidly and ingeniouſly ſuppoſes, that Mr. Theobald was not aware that the clauſe of the ſentence ſerved for the antecedent. Mr. Tyrrwhit very improperly taxes Theobald with pertneſs; he recommends the old reading, and fortifies it from

from an explanation of the French verb *défaire*. I muſt confeſs that Theobald's *defend* anſwers the purpoſe of the reader and auditor much better than the old word *defeat*, which cannot be maintained without much ſubtlety of argument. However the critics may determine, I would adviſe the actor to retain *defend*, as more intelligible to an audience.

LAFEU.

I think thou waſt created for men to breathe themſelves upon.

Lafeu is not very nice in the choice of terms to expreſs his ſcorn and contempt of Parolles. ' Breathe upon' is to be underſtood in the ſame ſenſe as a ſpeech of Prince Henry to Poins, concerning the tavern-waiters, act 2d of Henry IV. Firſt Part:

And, when you breathe in your watering, they cry hem! and bid you play it off.

Act III. Scene V.

HELEN.

I thank you, and will wait upon your leifure.

An ufual phrafe of civility in Shakfpeare's time, and explains a paffage in Hamlet, act the 3d:

The players wait upon your patience.

Act IV. Scene II.

DIANA.

'Tis not the many oaths that make the truth,
But the plain fimple vow that is vow'd true.
What is not holy, that we fwear not by,
But take the High'ft to witnefs; then, pray you, tell me,
If I fhould fwear by Jove's great attributes, &c.

In the explanation of thefe lines, much has been faid by the commentators. Mr. Steevens has, from the revifal, judicioufly fupported the text. Perhaps a fhort interpretation of Diana's intention may fatisfy the

the common reader better than a more learned diſcuſſion :

'The multitude of oaths prove nothing. That vow alone is valuable which is founded on truth and ſanctified by religion. Could you poſſibly believe me, though I ſhould appeal to heaven for the truth of what I uttered, when, at the ſame time, I was acting againſt my honour and my conſcience?'

DIANA.

Since Frenchmen are ſo *braid.*

The word *braid*, I believe, means *practiſed*, *accuſtomed*, or *beaten to a thing*. —— 'Bray a fool in a mortar.'

BERTRAM.

By an *abſtract* of ſucceſs.

That is, 'by an *abſtract*, or *memorandum*, of what I have taken down ſucceſſively in order.' So, in the Merry Wives of Windſor, Mrs. Ford tells Falſtaff, who wants to hide himſelf in her apartment, that her husband keeps an *abstract* of every thing that is in that chamber.

IDEM.

The business is not done, as fearing to hear of it hereafter.

Bertram means his intrigue with Diana. 'If the consequence of our meeting should be a child, I may chance to be called upon to maintain it.'

IDEM.

Entertained my convoy.

'Made a bargain with the men who are to attend me in my journey, and take care of my baggage, &c.'

BERTRAM.

I *con him* no thanks for this.

'Con him' is a Scottish phrase, and still in use.

IDEM.

He is a *cat* still.

Bertram calls him a *cat* three times, as a mark of great and incurable aversion.

All

All his phraſes of that kind are to be underſtood as in the Jew's liſt of antipathies in the Merchant of Venice:

Some that are mad if they behold a *cat*.

PAROLLES.

He will ſteal eggs out of a cloiſter.

This has the ſame meaning as to 'rob the 'ſpital.'

IDEM.

Faith, ſir, he has led the drum before the Engliſh tragedians.

It was formerly cuſtomary with the Engliſh itinerant players, and perhaps peculiar to them, to announce the play by beat of drum, and at the ſame time to diſtribute bills of the play to the populace.

PAROLLES, SOLUS.

Yet am I thankful. If my heart were great,
'Twould burſt at this. Captain I'll be no more.

This ſcene always afforded much pleaſure to the audience. Upon its laſt revival, it was acted with ſuch theatrical ſkill as excited general merriment. The unbinding Parolles, who looked about him with anxious ſurprize and terror, redoubled the burſts of laughter which echoed round the theatre. Woodward was excellent in the whole ſcene, but particularly in characterizing Bertram and the Dumaines, whoſe feelings, upon the unexpected heap of ſlander which he threw upon them, ſerved to heighten the ſcene. Bertram was moſt angry, becauſe Parolles deviated very little from the truth in what he ſaid of him; his laſciviouſneſs, and his intrigue with Diana, he could not deny.

In all our comic writers, I know not where to meet with ſuch an odd compound of cowardice, folly, ignorance, pertneſs, and effrontery, with certain ſemblances of courage, ſenſe, knowledge, adroitneſs, and wit, as Parolles. He is, I think, inferior only to the great maſter of ſtage gaiety and mirth, Sir John Falſtaff.

Beſſus,

Beſſus, in the King and no King of Beaumont and Fletcher, is, I know, highly extolled, as a great original, by ſome writers; and particularly by Mr. Seward, a very able commentator upon Beaumont and Fletcher, as a character ſecond only to the inimitable Fat Knight.

That Beſſus might, in his own days, be eſteemed as a juſt portrait of an impudent boaſter and a blaſted coward, and one who profeſſed to fight according to the rules of Caranza and Saviolino, thoſe great adepts in the art of challenging and fighting, I ſhall not deny; but this I will venture to ſay, that he is ſo widely different from any character we ſee at preſent, that no comic poet of this age will undertake his revival, even with conſiderable alterations; he is ſo outrageouſly diſtorted, in every limb and feature, that nothing but a new creation will do for Beſſus.

Soon after his preſent majeſty's acceſſion, Mr. Garrick intended to have brought forward to the public the King and no King of of Beaumont and Fletcher. Beſſus was given to Woodward; the manager deſigned Arbaces for himſelf. They both appeared to be much pleaſed with the proſpect of giving the public diverſion, and gaining great applauſe in the repreſentation of two characters new to the ſtage. And, doubtleſs, the quick tranſitions, from ſudden anger and violent rage to calm repentance and tame ſubmiſſion, in Arbaces, could not have been diſplayed with equal ſkill by any actor but Garrick; though a character, which is all paſſion and all repentance, is like a picture without keeping: the light and ſhade, though ſtrong, receive no advantage from the perſpective: the diſtreſs of Arbaces is, from ſituation, continually bordering upon the ridiculous.

The abſurdity, baſeneſs, and cowardice, of Beſſus, could not have been better diſpoſed of, perhaps, than to Harry Woodward. The other parts were diſtributed to advantage; the play was curtailed of ſuch ſcenes as were ſuppoſed to be ſuperfluous, and

and in ſome places altered and improved. But, however eager the manager was to bring out this play at firſt, it was obſerved, that, at every reading of it in the green-room, his pleaſure, inſtead of increaſing, ſuffered a viſible diminution. His uſual vivacity at laſt forſook him; he looked grave and ſtroked his chin, which, to the courtiers amongſt the players, who knew their monarch was his own miniſter, was a convincing ſign of his being diſſatisfied with the buſineſs that was going forward. At length he fairly gave up the deſign of acting King and no King; the parts were withdrawn from the actors, and no more was heard of it.

The cauſe of this ſudden reſolution was not known, though the conjectures concerning it were various. Some thought the title carried an objection. The words, King and no King, they ſaid, would make an odd appearance in the bills, more eſpecially as a young and beloved prince had juſt aſcended the throne of his anceſtors. Others

Others thought the impropriety of the ſtory, on which the play was founded, was a great defect; but this objection could have ſmall weight, as the plots of almoſt all our old dramatiſts are built upon romances, or hiſtories of very little credit.

Two reaſons, above all others, I believe, prevailed on the manager to drop this play. The King's ſtrange and contradictory agitations of mind are no otherwiſe to be accounted for than from his ardent paſſion to a lady whom he ſuppoſes to be his ſiſter: this belief raiſes him ſometimes to fits of frenzy. A play, founded upon inceſt, or any thing repugnant to nature, even in ſuppoſition, can never pleaſe an Engliſh audience. —— Why is Dryden's Don Sebaſtian almoſt baniſhed our theatres? The progreſs of the play, to a glorious fourth act, promiſes a noble cataſtrophe. In the fifth act, the two lovers, Sebaſtian and Almeyda, are diſcovered to be brother and ſiſter. After exchanging amorous glances and warm wiſhes, approaching to laſciviouſneſs, in the rich

rich eloquence of Dryden's harmonious verſes, they are obliged to part for ever. The Unnatural Combat of Maſſinger, one of his moſt finiſhed pieces, is for ever excluded the theatre for a like reaſon. Smith's Phædra and Hippolitus was coldly entertained, at the firſt acting of it, with all the powers of Betterton and Booth, Barry and Oldfield, to ſupport it; and could never win upon an audience in a revival.

But another very powerful reaſon for not acting King and no King prevailed, I am perſuaded, with a man of Garrick's reflection. He did not chooſe to hazard the obtruding ſuch a character on the public as Beſſus, who, though a captain in the army, is not only a beaten and diſgraced coward, but a voluntary pandar; a wretch who offers to procure a lady for the king his maſter, ſuppoſed, by him, to be his own ſiſter; and, not ſatisfied with this degree of infamy, by way of ſupererogation, he declares he would not ſcruple to go on the ſame ſcandalous errand to the king's mother.

ther. This fellow is a rare ſecond to Jack Falſtaff, for ſo we are informed in the animated lines of Mr. Colman to Philaſter:

Beaumont and Fletcher, thoſe twin ſtars that run
Their glorious courſe round Shakſpeare's golden ſun:
Or when Philaſter Hamlet's place ſupply'd,
Or Beſſus walk'd with Falſtaff by his ſide.

As cowardice, in the abſtract, is a bad ſubject of ridicule, ſo is the wretch who is employed to raiſe the mirth of an audience by being often kicked. Can we laugh at him, who, when completely drubbed, ſays, '*That ſufferance has made me wainſcot.*'

Humanity muſt be ſhocked at this as well as what follows: '*There is not a rib in his body that has not been thrice broken with dry beating, and now his ſides look like two wicker-targets, every way bended.*' King and no King. Act IV.

This may be wit, but it is of the blunteſt ſort I ever met with; but, as if this was not ſufficient, after the theatre has echoed with the mirth reſulting from the two ſevere drubbings of this ſecond Falſtaff,

ſtaff, in a ſubſequent ſcene he is twinged by the noſe, kicked, beaten, and trod upon.

What muſt we think of an audience that could be diverted with ſuch hyperbolical ſtuff, and ſuch cruel treatment of a poor miſerable wretch, after having been delighted with the truly diverting ſcenes of a Parolles and a Falſtaff? This ſurely is being

'Sated with celeſtial food, and feeding upon garbage.'

It is more to be wondered Mr. Garrick could have any thoughts of reviving King and no King, than that he ſhould afterwards withdraw it.

It had been ſaid that Mr. Garrick had once made a promiſe to a gentleman, reſpectable for elegance of taſte and politeneſs of manners, to act Arbaces and Beſſus alternately. This promiſe muſt have been made when Roſcius was in a very gay humour; or, at leaſt, much off his guard.

The cowards of Shakſpeare are not rendered ſo abſolutely unfit for all ſociety as Beſſus

Beſſus and his companions, the ſwordſmen; fellows who gravely take meaſure of a man's ſhoe to diſcover by that whether the owner had kicked a fellow into diſgrace or not. Though we ſhould grant that Parolles, in real life, would not be a very eligible companion, yet, I believe, no audience would refuſe his acquaintance. Beaumont and Fletcher place their cowards in ſuch ſituations as muſt produce nothing but contempt and diſguſt. Parolles fetches out rich matter, fine ſpleen, and choleric humour, from old Lafeu. His diſtreſs, when blinded, is of the moſt whimſical ſort, and the acute invention of his anſwers, to the interpreter's interrogatories, afford perpetual laughter.

Even, in his laſt ſtage of Tom Drum, when he is produced as an evidence againſt Bertram, the rogue is ſo characteriſtically diverting that you cannot find in your heart to be very angry; you almoſt pardon him, and wiſh he were taken into favour again. The generous Lafeu is half inclined to it, and,

and, that he is made ſo relenting, we muſt attribute to our author's great knowledge of man and *his large nature*, as Ben Jonſon expreſſes it. He knew that thoſe who are moſt prone to vehement anger are the ſooneſt pacified. Hot ſpirits make quicker haſte to repair the miſchiefs of their eſcapes from reaſon, than thoſe who are more temperate and ſedate.

Act V. Scene III.

KING.

For we are old, and, on our quickeſt decrees,
The inaudible and noiſeleſs foot of time
Steals ere we can effect them.

Dr. Johnſon, in his life of Pope, has an excellent thought on the unconquerable power of time: 'He that runs againſt time has an antagoniſt not ſubject to caſualties.'

IDEM.

This ring was mine, and, when I gave it Helen,
I bade her, if her fortune ever ſtood
Neceſſitated to help, that, by this token,
I would relieve her.———

This is ſo like the circumſtance of Queen Elizabeth's giving a ring to the Earl of Eſſex, with the ſame kind intention, in behalf of that unfortunate nobleman, that I cannot help thinking that our author inſerted it, in his play, from that well-known fact. I am aware that All's well that ends well was firſt acted in 1598, though not printed till 1623: but our author, it is known, frequently made alterations and additions to ſeveral of his pieces.

LAFEU.

I will buy me a ſon-in-law in a fair, and toll for this.

' I will rather go to a country fair, where I ſhall have my choice of peaſants or country clowns, and pick out a ſon from them, than marry my daughter to ſo worthleſs a fellow as this, whoſe knell I would moſt willingly ring.' I do not preſume to give this as the infallible meaning of the paſſage in queſtion; but it is ſurely very probable.

BERTRAM.

[*Speaking of Parolles.*] —— What of him?
He's *quoted* for a moſt perfidious ſlave,
With all the ſpots o'th' world tax'd and deboſh'd.

Mr. Steevens ſays, rightly, that *quoted* has the ſame ſenſe as *noted*; but, in this particular place, it bears, I think, a yet ſtronger meaning. 'He is ſtigmatiſed as a well-known and moſt abhorred liar.'

King John's reproach to Hubert contains a fuller interpretation of this word than Polonius's 'quoted him,' in Hamlet:

——— Hadſt not thou been by,
A fellow, by the hand of nature mark'd,
Quoted, and ſign'd to do a deed of ſhame,—&c.

Every Man in his Humour.

CHAPTER XXIII.

Particular merit of Every Man in his Humour. — *Ben Jonson's language.* — *Kitely and Bobadil.—Master Stephen and Slender.* —*Clement, Downright, and Brainworm.* —*Knowell.* — *Anecdote of Shakspeare and Jonson.* — *Prologue to* Every Man in his Humour. — *Jonson's malice.* — *Dennis's thunder.* — *This comedy revived after the Restoration.* — *Account of its revival.*— *Lord Dorset's prologue.* — *Mistake of Downs.—Medburne and the popish plot.*— Every Man in his Humour *revived by Garrick.* — *Merit of the several actors.*— *Some account of the dead and living.* — *Anecdote of Garrick and Woodward.* — *Mrs. Ward, Delane, and Garrick.—Messieurs Smith, Palmer, Dodd, and Baddeley,*

ley, commended.— Henderſon.— Every man out of his humour. — Dr. Hurd and Carlo Buffone.—Definition of humour.—*Jonſon's panegyric of Queen Elizabeth. — His poetaſter.—Quarrel with the players.—Whom he ſatirizes.—Conjectures concerning them.*

EVERY Man in his Humour is founded on ſuch follies and paſſions as are perpetually incident to, and connected with, man's nature; ſuch as do not depend upon local cuſtom or change of faſhion; and, for that reaſon, will bid fair to laſt as long as many of our old comedies. The language of Jonſon is very peculiar; in perſpicuity and elegance he is inferior to Beaumont and Fletcher, and very unlike the maſculine dialogue of Maſſinger. It is almoſt needleſs to obſerve that he comes far ſhort of the variety, ſtrength, and natural flow, of Shakſpeare. To avoid the common idiom, he plunges into ſtiff, quaint, and harſh, phraſeology: he has borrowed more words, from the Latin tongue, than all the authors of his time. However, the ſtyle of this play, as well as that of the Alchemiſt and Silent Woman, is more diſentangled and free from foreign auxiliaries than the greateſt part of his works. Moſt of the characters are truly dramatic: Kitely, though not equal to Ford in The Merry Wives of Windſor, who can plead a more juſtifiable cauſe of jealouſy, is yet well conceived, and is placed ſo artfully in ſituation, as to draw forth a conſiderable ſhare of comic diſtreſs.

Bobadil is an original. The coward, aſſuming the dignity of calm courage, was, I believe, new to our ſtage; at leaſt, I can remember nothing like him. From Bobadil, Congreve formed his Noll Bluff; a part moſt admirably acted by Ben Jonſon the comedian. Maſter Stephen is an honeſter object of ridicule than maſter Slender. One is nature's oaf, conſequently rather an object of compaſſion than ſcorn. The other is a fop of faſhion, and the gulled imitator of the follies which he admires

mires in his companions. Clement and Downright are ſtrongly marked with humour, eſpecially the firſt; and Brainworm is a fellow of merry and arch contrivance. In drawing this character, I believe the author had Terence, or rather, Plautus, of whom he was acknowledged to be an imitator, in his eye. Wellbred and young Knowell are diſtinguiſhed by no peculiarities. Old Knowell is ſomething like the anxious Simo of Terence.

A remarkable anecdote, concerning the introduction of this play to the theatre, has been handed down traditionally. Ben Jonſon preſented his Every Man in his Humour to one of the leading players in that company of which Shakſpeare was a member. After caſting his eye over it careleſſly and ſuperciliouſly, the comedian was on the point of returning it to the author with a peremptory refuſal; when Shakſpeare, who perhaps had never, till that inſtant, ſeen Jonſon, deſired he might look into the play. He was ſo well pleaſed with it, on perufal, that he recommended the work and the author to his fellows. The fuccefs of the comedy was confiderable, and we find that the principal actors were employed in it; Burbage, Kempe, Hemmings, Condell, and Sly. Shakfpeare himfelf is generally faid, by his name being firft in the drama, to have acted the part of old Knowell. He was, at that time, in the thirty-fourth year of his age, and Ben Jonfon in his twenty-fourth.

Notwithftanding the friendfhip which Shakfpeare had manifefted to Ben, by patronizing his play, yet the reader will find that the prologue is nothing lefs than a fatirical picture of feveral of Shakfpeare's dramas, particularly his Henry V. and the three parts of Henry VI. I am of opinion, too, that Lear and the Tempeft are pointed at in the following lines:

Nor creaking throne comes down the boys to pleafe,
Nor nimble fquib is feen to make afeard
The gentlewomen, nor roll'd bullet heard
To fay it thunders, nor tempeftuous drum
Rumbles to tell you when the ftorm is come.

These

Theſe lines may indeed apply, as the editor of Jonſon hinted to me, to other writers as well as Shakſpeare, but, as they follow other lines, unqueſtionably hoſtile to him, I cannot avoid believing that he levelled the whole principally at the man whom he moſt envied.

The playhouſe thunder was compoſed of much the ſame materials in Queen Beſs's days as in the reign of George III. I never heard of any improvement in the theatrical artillery of the ſky, if we except that ſort of which Mr. Dennis claimed the invention; but whether he mixed any particular ingredients in the bullet, or ordered that a greater number of them ſhould be rolled in a particular direction, or whether he contrived a more capacious thunder-bowl, I am really at a loſs for information; but, ſo jealous was he leſt his art of making thunder ſhould be imparted to others, without his conſent, that, Mr. Pope informs us, he cried out vehemently, at ſome tragedy, upon on hearing an uncommon burſt of thunder, "By G— that's my thunder." Whether the ſame critic invented the repreſentation of heavy ſhowers of theatrical rain, by rattling a vaſt quantity of peas in rollers, I am equally ignorant.

Every Man in his Humour was firſt publiſhed in 1602. The prologue was not added to that edition of the play, nor muſt we ſuppoſe that it was ſpoken originally; and, indeed, ſuch a groſs affront to their great friend would not have been permitted by the players. I do not think that this inſolent invective was ever pronounced on the ſtage, nor printed, till after the death of Shakſpeare, who died in April, 1616, which, according to the then reckoning of time, was ſoon after the beginning of the year. Jonſon collected his works into one volume in the ſame year, and took that opportunity of indulging his poſthumous malice, by fixing this introduction to his firſt play. This is of a piece with his general conduct through his whole life

to

to Shakſpeare. When he ſat down to write a panegyric *on his beloved*, prefixed to his works, as he there calls Shakſpeare, he muſt, for a time, have purged his brain and heart of all ſpleen, envy, and malevolence: for a more accurate or extenſive eulogium, on the genius and writings of Shakſpeare, could not well be conceived.

Amongſt the old plays revived, upon the opening of the theatres after the Reſtoration, this comedy was not forgotten. It was acted, as I conjecture, about the year 1675, by the duke of York's company, in Dorſet Gardens. Not having met with a printed copy of the play, as then acted, I cannot eaſily divine how the parts were divided. In all probability, Betterton, Smith, Harris, Nokes, Underhill, and ſome others of the prime comedians, were employed in it.

A taſte for Jonſon was endeavoured to be revived: though, I believe, that was always an up-hill work; and in this belief I am confirmed from ſome ſhrewd reflections

tions thrown out by L. Diggs, in a copy of verſes prefixed to Shakſpeare's poems. However, the recommendation was ſo powerful, that it amounted to a command. The Earl of Dorſet favoured the players with an epilogue, from which we learn that the parts were well fitted. It contains ſome ſtage anecdotes or hiſtory which may not be diſpleaſing to the readers, more eſpecially as Lord Dorſet's works, ſeparately printed, are not to be met with.

Epilogue on the revival of Ben Jonſon's play, called Every Man in his Humour.

[*The actor is ſuppoſed to enter with reluctance.*]

Intreaty ſhall not ſerve, nor violence,
To make me ſpeak in ſuch a play's defence.
A play, where wit and humour do agree
To break all practis'd laws of comedy.
The ſcene, what more abſurd! in England lies:
No gods deſcend; no dancing devils riſe:
No captive prince from unknown country brought;
No battle; nay, there's ſcare a duel fought.

And

And ſomething yet more ſharply might be ſaid,
But I conſider the poor author's dead;
Let that be his excuſe,——now for our own:
Why,——faith, in my opinion, we need none.
The parts were fitted well; but ſome will ſay
Pox on them, rogues! what made them take this
play!
I do not doubt but you will credit me;
It was not choice, but mere neceſſity.
To all our writing friends in town we ſent,
But not a wit durſt venture out in Lent:
Have patience but till Eaſter Term, and then
You ſhall have jog and hobby-horſe again.
Here's Maſter Matthew, our domeſtic wit,
Does promiſe one o' th' ten plays he has writ.
But, ſince great bribes weigh nothing with the juſt,
Know we have merits, and to them we truſt.
When any faſts or holidays defer
The public labours of the theatre,
We ride not forth, although the day be fair,
On ambling tit, to take the ſuburb air;
But with our authors meet, and ſpend that time
To make up quarrels between ſenſe and rhyme.
Wedneſdays and Fridays conſtantly we ſat;
Till, after many a long and free debate,
For divers weighty reaſons, 'twas thought fit,
Unruly ſenſe ſhould ſtill to rhyme ſubmit.
This the moſt glorious law we ever made,
So ſtrictly in this epilogue obey'd,

Sure

Sure no man here will ever dare to break.

[*Enter Jonſon's ghoſt, who, by action, removes the ſpeaker of the former part of the epilogue.*]

Hold, and give way, for I myſelf will ſpeak ;
Can you encourage ſo much inſolence,
And add new faults ſtill to the great offence
Your anceſtors ſo raſhly did commit
Againſt the mighty powers of art and wit,
When they condemn'd thoſe noble works of mine,
Sejanus, and my beſt love, Catiline.
Repent, or on your guilty heads ſhall fall
The curſe of many a rhyming paſtoral.
The three bold Beauchamps ſhall revive again,
And with the London 'Prentice conquer Spain.
All the dull follies of the former age
Shall find applauſe on this corrupted ſtage.
But, if you pay the great arrears of praiſe,
So long ſince due to my much-injur'd plays,
From all paſt crimes I firſt will ſet you free,
And then inſpire ſome one to write like me.

Downs, in a liſt of plays acted by the king's company at Drury-lane, has placed Every Man in his Humour. I, at firſt, ſuppoſed that it had been revived by the comedians of that houſe ; but Medbourne being taken notice of in the epilogue, as the domeſtic poet of the playhouſe, who

was

was an actor in the duke's company, I am convinced that our ſtage-hiſtorian was in an error, or that this play was revived at both theatres, contrary to an eſtabliſhed order of the court, which enjoined the two theatres to divide the old plays between them, and not meddle with one another's property.

Matthew Medbourne, who, in this epilogue, is ſaid to have had no leſs than ten plays by him, was an excellent actor. He rendered himſelf acceptable, by his learning and accompliſhments, to perſons of faſhion and taſte, and was particularly diſtinguiſhed by the earl of Dorſet, who, not only condeſcended to mention him in this epilogue, but wrote an epilogue to his tranſlation of Moliere's Tartuffe. Medbourne lived at a time when the ſtate diviſions were at the height. He was a Roman Catholic, and warmly attached to the intereſt of his royal patron the duke of York. Unhappily, perhaps, on account of ſome imprudent expreſſion, or for ſome inadvertent behaviour,

viour, he was involved in the popiſh plot, and thrown into Newgate, where he was ſuffered to periſh. Such was the rage of party, that a man of ſo little conſequence as a player was made an object of popular reſentment by the furious politics of Lord Shaftſbury and his colleagues.

I was informed, many years ſince, that Every Man in his humour was revived at the theatre in Lincoln's-inn-fields about the year 1720: how the parts were diſtributed I could not learn.

Towards the beginning of the year 1750, Mr. Garrick was induced, by his own judgement, or the advice of others, to revive this comedy, and to bring it on his ſtage. He expunged all ſuch paſſages in it as either retarded the progreſs of the plot, or, through length of time, were become obſolete or unintelligible; and theſe were not a few. Of all our old playwrights, Jonſon was moſt apt to allude to local cuſtoms and temporary follies. Mr. Garrick likewiſe added a ſcene of his own.

Notwithſtanding

Notwithſtanding all the care he had beſtowed in pruning and dreſſing this dramatic tree, he was fearful it would not flouriſh when brought forth to public view. To prevent, therefore, any miſcarriage in the acting of the play, he took an accurate ſurvey of his company, and conſidered their diſtinct and peculiar faculties. He gave to each comedian a part which he thought was in the compaſs of his power to hit off with ſkill. Kitely, the jealous huſband, which requires great art in the performer, he took upon himſelf; to Woodward he aſſigned Bobadil, which has been thought, by many good judges, to have been his maſterpiece in low comedy. Brainworm was played with all the archneſs and varied pleaſantry that could be aſſumed by Yates: Welbred and Young Knowell by Roſs and Palmer. Shuter entered moſt naturally into the follies of a young, ignorant, fellow, who thinks ſmoking tobacco faſhionably, and ſwearing a ſtrange kind of oath, the higheſt proofs of humour and tafte. Winftone, who was tolerated in other parts, in Downright was highly applauded. Old Knowell became the age and perfon of Berry. Mrs. Ward, a pretty woman, and an actrefs of confiderable talents, acted dame Kitely. Mifs Minors, fince Mrs. Walker, was the Mrs. Bridget. I muft not forget mafter Matthew, the town gull, which was given, with much propriety, to Harry Vaughan, a brother of Mrs. Pritchard, a man formed by nature for fmall parts of low humour and bufy impertinence; fuch as Tefter in the Sufpicious Hufband, Simple in the Merry Wives of Windfor, and Simon in the Apprentice.

After all the attention of the acting manager to draw together fuch a groupe of original actors as were fcarce ever collected before, the antiquated phrafe of old Ben appeared fo ftrange, and was fo oppofite to the tafte of the audience, that he found it no eafy matter to make them relifh the play. However, by obftinate

perfeverance,

perſeverance, and by retrenching every thing that hurt the ear or diſpleaſed the judgement, he brought it, at laſt, to be a favourite dramatic diſh, which was often preſented to full and brilliant audiences.

Not any of the actors, who figured in in this comedy, are now living, except Mr. Yates, Mr. Roſs, and Miſs Minors. To what I have ſaid of thoſe who are dead, I ſhall now only add, that Palmer, who married Miſs Pritchard, died by an improper draught given him, in his illneſs, through miſtake. Harry Vaughan, by fancying himſelf co-heir with his ſiſter, Mrs. Pritchard, to large property, which was conteſted by other claimants, (the heirs at law,) exchanged a life of innocence and eaſe for much diſappointment and vexation of mind. He died rich, but neither happy nor reſpected. However, I believe he thought that he had a right to that of which he had acquired poſſeſſion.

The frequent rehearſal of this comedy was a convincing proof of Garrick's great anxiety for its public approbation. As no man more perfectly knew the various characters of the drama than himſelf, his reading a new or revived piece was a matter of inſtruction, as well as entertainment, to the players. He generally ſeaſoned the dry part of the lecture with acute remarks, ſhrewd applications to the company preſent, or ſome gay jokes, which the comedians of the theatre, who ſurvive their old maſter, will recollect with pleaſure.

As he took infinite pains to inform, he expected an implicit ſubmiſſion to his inſtructions. A compliance, after all, which could not be expected from men of great profeſſional abilities, ſuch as Yates and Woodward. All that can be expected from genius is, to take the out-line and to obſerve a few hints towards the colouring of a character; the heightening, or finiſhing, muſt be left to the performer.

During

During the greateſt part of the rehearſals of Every Man in his Humour, Woodward ſeemed very attentive to Garrick's ideas of Bobadil. But, in his abſence one morning, he indulged himſelf in the exhibition of his own intended manner of repreſentation. While the actors were laughing and applauding Woodward, Garrick entered the playhouſe, and, unperceived, attended to the tranſaction of the ſcene. After waiting ſometime, he ſtept on the ſtage, and cried, " Bravo, Harry! bravo! upon my ſoul, bravo!—Why, now this is—no, no, I can't ſay this is quite my idea of the thing—Yours is, after all—to be ſure, rather—ha!" — Woodward perceiving the manager a little embarraſſed, with much ſeeming modeſty, ſaid, " Sir, I will act the part, if you deſire it, exactly according to your notion of it."—" No, no! by no means, Harry. D—n it, you have actually clenched the matter.—But why, my dear Harry, would not you communicate before."

Mrs. Ward was a very favourite actreſs at Edinburgh, when Delane and Sparks exhibited upon the theatre of that city, in the ſummer of 1748. Delane, though at that time in the ſervice of Mr. Garrick, perhaps inadvertently recommended her to his old maſter, Mr. Rich, who immediately fixed her in his company by articles of agreement. Her firſt appearance, at Covent-Garden theatre, was in Cordelia, the winter enſuing, when Quin acted Lear.

Though this actreſs was very attractive in feature and agreeable in figure, yet, it muſt be granted, that parts of vigour and loftineſs were much more ſuitable to her manner than Cordelia. The high paſſions of Hermione were more congenial to her voice and ſpirit than a Shore or a Monimia: ſhe was a better Caliſta than a Juliet. She died about twelve years ſince. Delane's complaiſance to Rich, by being an inſtrument of engaging, to that manager, Mrs. Ward, loſt him the friendſhip of Garrick, and occaſioned a quarrel between

them

them which ended only with the life of the former. Before this tranſaction, they had been on the moſt friendly terms: Garrick had publicly profeſſed himſelf the friend of Delane, and took a pleaſure in walking with him, in the ſtreet, arm in arm. But, '*O world, thy ſlippery turns!*'* Delane, ſoon after his arrival from Scotland, accidentally met Garrick in the piazza of Covent-Garden, who not only would not return his ſalute, but gave him ſuch a look of anger and diſdain as few men, beſides himſelf, had it in their power to beſtow. An immediate ſeparation of intereſt enſued. Delane's articles were given up, and he was hired to Mr. Rich. This actor did not long ſurvive the quarrel. He was a man of ſpirit, and felt all the diſagreeableneſs of contemptuous treatment. Whether, in conſequence of this difference, he applied himſelf with greater eagerneſs to his bottle, or whether it was

* Coriolanus.

owing to his ufual indulgence in the circulation of the glafs, it was univerfally faid that he died a martyr to Bacchus. This happened about the year 1750.

Every Man in his Humour, notwithftanding the lofs of fo many capital performers, who played in it on its revival, continues ftill to be a play to which the public pays attention. Many of the characters are well adapted to the abilities of the actors, particularly Mr. Smith in Kitely, who, in this part, is not an unworthy fucceffor of our great Rofcius; Mr. Palmer in Bobadil, Mr. Dodd in Mafter Stephen, and Baddeley in Brainworm, are much approved. Their merit appears to greater advantage, as they could not have the fame inftructions which their predeceffors had. Mr. Henderfon, when at Drury-lane, tried his fkill in Bobadil. Though different in his manner from Woodward, he drew a good portrait of the coward and the bully. —Were he to act it oftener, he would certainly be more warm in his colouring.

The

The ſucceſs of Every Man in his Humour encouraged Ben to write Every Man out of his Humour. This he, very judiciouſly, I think, calls a comic ſatire. It conſiſts of a variety of characters, exhibiting manners rather in looſe and independent ſcenes than in a regular fable. Downs places this comedy in the liſt of plays which were revived by the king's company of comedians. But I believe he is guilty of the ſame miſtake which he fell into with reſpect to Every Man in his Humour, which I have ſufficiently proved was acted by Betterton's company. Whether Ben Jonſon was the firſt dramatiſt who introduced upon our ſtage a grex, who comment upon the action of the ſeveral characters in the play, is not very material. He has been followed in this by the Duke of Buckingham and others, and by Mr. Foote lately in ſome of his farces, in which ſome of his actors have ſpoken to others on the ſtage from the

the gallery and the boxes, to the no ſmall entertainment of the ſpectators. This piece has, in my opinion, a great ſhare of comic pleaſantry, and, with ſome judicious alterations, would now afford rational amuſement. Some of the characters, it is true, are obſolete through age; others, ſuch as the Envious Man and the Paraſite, are of all times and all nations. Macilente and Carlo Buffone will laſt till doomſday: they are admirably well drawn. The objection of Dr. Hurd, who terms the play a hard delineation of a groupe of ſimply-exiſting paſſions, wholly chimerical, is ill-founded. Some of theſe parts are to be ſeen now in ſome ſhape or other; faſhionable ſhadows of foppery and cuſtom vary with times and circumſtances. Who does not ſee every day a Sogliardo and Fungoſo, differently modified, in our metropolis at this inſtant? In a rude unpoliſhed age, when the people were juſt emancipated from barbariſm by the renovation of literature and the light of reformation, a groupe of new and abſurd

ſurd characters muſt naturally ſpring up which would furniſh ample materials of ridicule to the comic writers; and who can deny that Jonſon has, in this play, laid hold of many growing follies of the times in which he lived?

With ſubmiſſion to ſo juſtly-celebrated a writer as Dr. Hurd, I would aſk, what is it that conſtitutes character? Is it not that diſtinguiſhed paſſion, or peculiar humour, which ſeparates a man from the reſt of his ſpecies? Characters are formed from manners, and theſe are derived from paſſions. When they are indulged to a certain diſtinguiſhing degree, ſo as to make a man ridiculous or remarkable, we then call him a character. The Muſes' Looking-Glaſs cannot be paralelled with Every Man in his Humour; becauſe in this we have action, which the other wants.

Jonſon has, in one part, delineated a character which did not exiſt perhaps in that full force in his own days, and with ſuch eclat and additional force from cer-

tain

tain circumſtances, as it has done ſince. Many ſtriking features of Carlo Buffone will, if I miſtake not, be acknowledged to have exiſted in a late ſhining comic genius. Let us read Buffone's character given by Cordato: ——

'*He is one whom the author calls Carlo Buffone, an impudent common jeſter, a violent railer, and an incomprehenſible epicure; one whoſe company is deſired of all men, but beloved of none; he will ſooner loſe his ſoul than a jeſt, and profane even the moſt holy things to excite laughter; no honourable or reverend perſonage whatſoever, that comes within the reach of his eye, but is turned into all manner of variety by his adulterous ſimilies.*'

We muſt grant Jonſon the merit of being the firſt who could fix that uncertain and wandering thing, called *humour*, by a juſt and accurate definition:

" —— When ſome peculiar quality
Doth ſo poſſeſs a man, that it doth draw
All affects, his ſpirits, and his powers,

In

In their conſtructions, all to run one way, —
This may be truly ſaid to be a *humour*."

This comic ſatire gave general ſatisfaction. Queen Elizabeth, drawn by the fame which was ſpread of it, honoured the play with her preſence. Jonſon, to pay a reſpectful compliment to his ſovereign, altered the concluſion of his play into an elegant panegyric, ſpoken by Malicente; which turns upon this ſimple idea; that her majeſty's powerful influence had converted him, the repreſentative of envy, into a contrary character. Mr. Collins, the author of ſeveral juſtly-eſteemed poems, firſt pointed out to me the particular beauties of this occaſional addreſs. The reader will not think his time ill ſpent in reading the moſt intereſting part of it:

— In the ample and unmeaſur'd flood
Of her perfections are my paſſions drown'd;
And I have now a ſpirit as ſweet and clear
As the moſt rarified and ſubtle air.
With which, and with a heart as pure as fire,
Yet humble as the earth, do I implore
Heaven, that ſhe, whoſe preſence hath effected

This

This change in me, may suffer most late change
In her admir'd and happy government.
May still this island be call'd fortunate!
And rugged treason tremble at the sound,
When fame shall speak it with an emphasis.
Let foreign polity be dull as lead,
And pale invasion come with half a heart,
When he looks upon her blessed soil.
The throat of war be stopp'd within her land,
And turtle-footed Peace dance fairy-rings
About her court; where never may there come
Suspect or danger, but all trust and safety!
Let Flattery be dumb, and Envy blind,
In her dread presence; Death himself admire her;
And may her virtues make him to forget
The use of his inevitable hand!
Fly from her, Age! Sleep, Time, before her throne!
Our strongest wall falls down when she is gone!

Macilente is the abstract of envy in Every Man out of his Humour; *Rancour*, in the *Roman comique* of Scarron, is the same character dilated. This play was acted, by the established comedians, in 1599. Why Jonson left them, and employed the children of the queen's chapel, in preference, to act his Cynthia's revels, is is a queſtion that cannot now be eaſily, if at all, decided.

We have ſome reaſon to conjecture, that the acting of Every Man in his Humour muſt have been attended with certain circumſtances unpleaſing to the author, or he would not have delivered his next play, '*As you find it,*' to be acted by children. This comedy, though worth ſaving from oblivion, does not call, in my opinion, for the eulogium which has been conferred upon it.

In his introduction to his Every Man out of his Humour, the author told the people, with more frankneſs than diſcretion, that, if they did not like his play, it muſt be attributed to their ignorance:

> ———————— If we fail,
> We muſt impute it to this only chance,—
> Art hath an enemy call'd ignorance.

In As you find it, he ſeems to complain of the rude behaviour of an audience, in manifeſting their diſlike and contempt, by various

various methods, to a good play; meaning, no doubt, one of his own. This charge he renewed. In his dialogue of the boys, at the beginning of Cynthia's Revels, and indeed almoſt through all his pieces, he ſeems to be exceedingly ſore; for he imprudently provokes the ill-will and contempt of thoſe who muſt finally condemn or eſtabliſh his works, and from whom there can be no adequate appeal. Shakſpeare modeſtly courted the good-will of his auditors; Jonſon defied and affronted them.

His next piece, the poetaſter, is a ſatire upon the players, under the pretence of retaliating the abuſe he had ſuffered from Decker. Notwithſtanding all he has ſaid to defend himſelf from the charge of general obloquy on the ſociety of actors, in a dialogue which he tells us was ſpoken but once, by way of addreſs to the audience, the poetaſter is a formal attack upon the comedians and their profeſſion. Churchill was a generous and fair ſatiriſt; Jonſon inſidiouſly

inſidiouſly ſkulks under the pretence of aiming at one or two of the fraternity, when he really levels his ſhafts at them all. Some of the players he characterizes under feigned names: ſuch as 'the lean Poluphagus,' by whom I conjecture he means Burbage, who, I have no doubt, acted the lean Macilente. Of him he makes Tucca ſay,—'He will eat a leg of mutton, while I am in my porridge. His belly is like Barathrum.' By 'Friſker the zany, and good ſkipping ſwaggerer,' I have fancied that he meant Kempe, who was celebrated for his ready wit and facetious jeſting: however, this is only conjecture. Who he means by 'Mango, the fat fool,' is ſtill leſs in my conception. 'You may bring him,' ſays Tucca, who is the author's mouth-piece againſt the comedians; 'but let him not beg rapiers and ſcarfes in his own familiar playing face, nor roar out his barren bold jeſts with a tormenting laughter between drunk and dry. Do you hear, Stifftoe?

give him warning to forſake his ſaucy glavering grace and his goggle eye; it does not become him, ſirrah!' Lowin was the original Falſtaff, and played innumerable parts of humour and pleaſantry: perhaps Ben flings this outrageous ſarcaſm at this actor. We have leave to gueſs any body, ſince he ſpares nobody.

The Poetaſter, notwithſtanding the author's predilection for it, is one of Jonſon's loweſt productions: it was conceived in malice and brought forth in anger. It is indeed a contemptible mixture of the ſerio-comic, where the names of Auguſtus Cæſar, Mecænas, Virgil, Horace, Ovid, and Tibullus, are all ſacrificed upon the altar of private reſentment. The tranſlations from the claſſics are meanly literal, as well as harſh and quaint, and far inferior to thoſe of Chapman, or any other tranſlator of thoſe times. Jonſon's Tucca is a wretched copy, or ape, of the inimitable Falſtaff. This comical ſatire, as it is called, cloſes with an apologetical addreſs to the reader, ſtuffed

with

with farther abuſe upon the players, with a ſlender exception in favour of *ſome better natures* amongſt them. There is nothing ſo remarkable in this dialogue as the author's arrogance. After having laboured moſt ſtrenuouſly to give proofs of his importance, in a kind of poetic rapture, he thruſts his friends from him, by telling them, ' He will try if Tragedy have a more kind aſpect, for her favours he will next purſue.' We muſt ſuppoſe, then, that he was in labour of his great Sejanus.

By the mediation of friends, and moſt likely by the good-offices of our gentle Shakſpeare, a reconciliation was effected between this ſurly writer and the comedians.

CHAPTER XXIV.

Jonſon's Sejanus.—Aſſiſted in it by Shakſpeare. — Sejanus inferior to Shakſpeare's third-rate tragedies.— Jonſon's tranſlations from the claſſics. — His ignorance of decency and decorum. — Defence of Silius commended.— Tiberius and Macro.— Soliloquy of Sejanus. — Catiline.— Condemned originally.— Revived by Charles Hart.— Suppoſed at the inſtigation of Buckingham, Dorſet, &c. — Cicero's ſpeeches immoderately long.— Cicero's character rejected, by Major Mohun, for Cethegus.— His excellence in the part.— Jonſon's ladies.— Leonard Digges. — His verſes on Jonſon's three comedies. — Jonſon's frown. — Acquainted with the Duke of Buckingham when the duke was a boy. — Stage-learning required for Jonſon's characters.

SHAKSPEARE not only acted a part in Sejanus, but wrote ſome ſcenes for it, as as originally reprefented. Of this Jonfon takes notice in an advertifement to an edition of this play printed in 1605; and, though he does not mention his coadjutor's name, he points him out by the appellation of a happy genius. However, it is remarkable, though he condefcended to be the avowed fellow-labourer of Chapman, Marfton, Rowley, and others, he affures the reader, with a fneer, that he would not join his own inferior matter to that of the great poet; but he wrote over again thofe fcenes which had been wrought into the piece by the pen of Shakfpeare. Who does not wifh that Shakfpeare had put as high a value upon his true brilliants as Ben did upon his jewels of pafte? The fcenes, rejected by Jonfon, Shakfpeare did not preferve. I have had fome little fufpicion, that Shakfpeare's part of this tragic entertainment might poffibly be that alone which efcaped public cenfure; the play, he tells us himfelf, was univerfally exploded. Nay, he fays that the body of Sejanus did

 not

not fare better from the Roman mob than the play did from the ſpectators.

Ben, notwithſtanding, greatly valued himſelf upon this tragedy. Let any candid judge examine it with the ſecond or third rate tragedies of Shakſpeare, and he will find it far inferior to the ſpirit that reigns in the worſt of them.

If, in his hiſtorical pieces, our admirable bard is ſometimes blameable for overloading his ſcenes with multiplicity of buſineſs, and with incidents undramatic, Ben Jonſon, in the ſelection of hiſtorical events, is far leſs happy than his rival. The ſpeeches of his principal characters are long and tedious, and neither intereſting from ſentiment, paſſion, or buſineſs. His tranſlations from the claſſics are tireſome and diſguſting, and retard, rather than forward, the progreſs of the play. When the tragedy is brought, by the death of Sejanus, to its proper period, (and which is pompouſly and too circumſtantially related from Juvenal,) the curtain is not

ſuffered

ſuffered to fall till you are tortured with, what might have been well ſpared, an odious relation of the cruel deaths of his young ſon, and his daughter, a child who is firſt vitiated by the common executioner, to be made a legal victim of juſtice to the ſtate. This man, the frequenter of courts, the ſcholar of Camden, the friend of Selden, and the companion of Sir Harry Savile, had no knowledge of decorum and decency.

But, that I may not be thought to view this author's writings with a partial malignity, let me candidly confeſs there is ſomething noble and affecting in the defence of Silius, whoſe voluntary death in the ſenate is ſtriking and truly dramatic; that Tiberius's diſſembled knowledge of Sejanus's deſigns, with his employing Macro to check the pride and inſolence of his minion, are maſterly touched; and the fine ſoliloquy of Sejanus, in which he enumerates the ſlaughter of his enemies, cannot be too much applauded.

To have done at once with Jonſon's tragic poetry, let us now proceed to his Catiline, which Lord Dorſet calls ' his beſt love, Catiline.'

We have the author's teſtimony that this play was condemned in the acting. It cannot now be known whether it was afterwards revived before the playhouſes were ſhut up in the beginning of the civil wars. I rather incline to think it muſt have been, by ſome means, brought again on the ſtage before the Reſtoration; ſome time after which it was revived by Charles Hart. — This great actor, having a conſiderable venture in the theatre, would not, without ſome proſpect of ſucceſs, have run the riſk of decorating a piece in which ſuch a number of characters were included.

The Duke of Buckingham and Lord Dorſet were admirers of Jonſon to a degree of idolatry; it is very probable, that, by liberal promiſes, they encouraged the actors to bring forward this forgotten tragedy. Certain it is, that the play was acted

acted ſeveral times during the reign of Charles II. The action of Hart, in Catiline, was univerſally applauded; and this contributed to keep alive what otherwiſe would have ſoon been loſt to be public. — 'Hart's action,' ſaid the great critic, Rymer, 'could throw a luſtre on the moſt wretched characters; and he ſo far dazzled the eyes of the ſpectator by it, that the deformities of the poet could not be diſcerned.' Jonſon has, beſides, placed Catiline in ſuch ſituations, and given ſentiments ſo correſpondent to his ambitious and ſavage mind, that a good actor could not fail to improve them to the delight of an intelligent audience. But, when we allow all this, and more, Catiline, upon the whole, is a very languid and tedious entertainment. Nothing but a very ſtrong prepoſſeſſion in the author's favour could have induced an audience to hear with patience the ſpeeches of Cicero, which, bating the interruptions of a line or two, are extended to the immeaſurable length

of

of one hundred and ſeventy lines. A great deal of Salluſt, and almoſt the whole of Cicero's Catilinarian orations, are tranſlated verbally. This, in Jonſon's age, was more unneceſſary perhaps than in our own: the claſſics were in every body's hands. The laſt editors of Shakſpeare have, with ſingular diligence, given a liſt of all the tranſlations from the Greek and Roman authors publiſhed in the reigns of Elizabeth and James; and it is almoſt aſtoniſhing to think what floods of ſcience and learning were poured in from theſe claſſic fountains.

The part of Cicero muſt have been an intolerable burden to an actor of Stentorian lungs, unleſs the orations were conſiderably curtailed. Major Mohun, who is celebrated by my Lord Rocheſter for the wonder of actors, rejected Cicero, and took a much ſhorter part, that of Cethegus, his acting of which the ſame nobleman much applauds. The manners of this play are, in one place particularly, more cenſurable

than

than thoſe of Sejanus. In the grand meeting of the conſpirators, one of them, by action, tempts a young lad to ſubmit to his infamous paſſion; upon his unwillingneſs to comply, Catiline threatens him with inſtant death if he perſiſts to refuſe gratifying the other's more than brutal inclination. This, I ſuppoſe, Ben would call the truth of hiſtory and highly characteriſtical. But ſurely he muſt have read and tranſlated Horace's Art of Poetry with little taſte who could be guilty of ſuch indecency. Jonſon's women are, in general, diſagreeable company; they are vicious and vulgar, and make the author ſmell too much of low company and the brothel. We have indeed one modeſt Celia, and my good Dame Kitely, to counterbalance his large number of rampant ladies. The ſcene, in Catiline, between Curius and Fulvia, by the conduct of which the conſpiracy is brought to light, is naturally imagined and dramatically conducted.—— Jonſon, by his knowledge of Roman manners,

ners, cuſtoms, attires, &c. avoids tolerably well the common fault of our old dramatiſts, who are ſure to travel with the manners of our metropolis to all parts of the globe.

The critics who lived in the ſame age with the author, and all who have ſucceeded till within theſe twenty or thirty years, have beſtowed the moſt ſuperlative commendations upon Volpone, the Silent Woman, and the Alchemiſt; and yet we find, by a contemporary, who ſeems to have no mean opinion of theſe comedies, that they were exhibited to empty benches, at a time when the name of Shakſpeare was a charm ſufficient to draw multitudes to ſee his dramatic works. Mr. Malone has quoted, in his Supplement to Shakſpeare, a copy of verſes, by Leonard Digges, prefixed to Shakſpeare's poems, where we have the following account of Jonſon's great chef-d'œuvres:

And,

And, though the Fox and ſubtle Alchemiſt,
Long intermitted, could not quite be miſs'd;
Though theſe have ſham'd the ancients, and might raiſe
Their author's merit with a crown of bays;
Yet theſe, ſometimes, ev'n at a friend's deſire,
Acted, have ſcarce defray'd the ſea-coal fire
And door-keepers:—when, let Falſtaff come,
Hal, Poins, the reſt,—you ſcarce ſhall have a room,
All is ſo peſter'd. Let but Beatrice
And Benedick be ſeen! lo! in a trice,
The cock-pit, gall'ries, boxes, all, are full, &c.

In another place of the ſame poem:

When, ſome new day, they would not brook a line
Of tedious, though well-labour'd, Catiline;
Sejanus, too, was irkſome ———

And this ſeems to be a fair and juſt account of the regard in which Jonſon was generally held. He was never ſupported by the public voice, though kept alive by the critics and the excellent performance of the actors. He had bullied the authors of his own times into an extraordinary opinion of his vaſt merit; and, when he died, he left ſuch a frown behind him, that

that he frightened all ſucceeding dramatic poets and critics, who were afraid to cenſure, what, in their hearts, they neither admired nor approved. I have already given my opinion that ſome of our leading nobility, and other court critics, made it their buſineſs to ſtimulate the players to revive their favourite author, though, I am perſuaded, the greateſt part of the audiences had no appetite for him. The duke of Buckingham has found room in his Rehearſal to give praiſe to Ben Jonſon, though he no where mentions Shakſpeare. But the duke, it ſeems, converſed with Ben when his grace was a boy of about thirteen, and the poet was near his grand climacterique, and thence conceived ſuch a veneration for him, that it never left him afterwards.

It was a conſtant complaint of the old actors, who lived in Queen Anne's time, that if Jonſon's plays were intermitted for a few years, they could not know how to perſonate his characters, they were ſo difficult, and their

manners

manners ſo diſtant, from thoſe of all other authors. To preſerve them required a kind of ſtage learning, which was traditionally hoarded up. Moſca, in Volpone, when he endeavours to work upon the avarice of Corvino, and to induce him to offer his wife to the pretendedly ſick voluptuary, pronounces the word *think*, ſeven or eight times: there is a difficulty ariſes here in various pauſe and difference of ſound. Many niceties of this kind were obſerved by the old comedians, which are now abſolutely loſt to the ſtage.

CHAP-

CHAPTER XXV.

Fable of Volpone. — Lucian's Dialogues.— Praise of The Fox.—The last act condemned. —The actors in Volpone. — Booth, Wilks, Cibber, Mills, Jonson.— Mrs. Clive.—Mr. Boman, &c.—Garrick's intention to revive Volpone. — The Silent Woman. — Revival in 1752. — Character of Morose. — Difficulty in acting Ben Jonson's characters. — His plays obsolete.—A sweet sonnet.—Cartwright and Mohun.—Respect paid by Booth, Wilks, and Cibber, to Jonson's Silent Woman.—Ben Jonson the actor.—Shepherd.— The Alchemist. — Bad catastrophe.— Abel Drugger. — The. Cibber. — Garrick and Weston. — Yates.—The two Palmers. — Ben Griffin and Ben Jonson. — Sir Epicure Mammon. — Harper and Love. — Doll Common. — Mrs. Clive and Mrs. Pritchard.

THE

THE Fable of Volpone is chosen with judgement, and is founded upon avarice and luxury. The paying obsequious and constant courtship to childless rich people, with a view to obtain from them bountiful legacies in return, has been a practice of all times, and in all nations. There is in Lucian, the father of true ridicule, an admirable dialogue, on this subject, between Pluto and Mercury. An old man of ninety is assiduously courted by several young fellows, who, in hopes of being his heirs, perform the lowest and meanest offices to him. Pluto orders Mercury to carry off these rascals, who are dividing, in their minds, the old fellow's riches, to the infernal shades, but commands him to double, nay, treble, the age of him who is the object of their obsequiousness. Lucian has no less than five or six dialogues on the same subject.

In the comedy of The Fox, there is not much to be censured, except the language, which is ſo pedantic and ſtuck ſo full of Latinity, that few, except the learned, can perfectly underſtand it. ' Jonſon, ſays Dr. Young, brought all the antients upon his head: by ſtudying to ſpeak like a Roman, he forgot the language of his country.'

The conduct of the plot in the firſt four acts, except the mountebank ſcene, is truly admirable. The laſt act is, in my opinion, quite farcical. That a man of Volpone's ſagacity ſhould venture to appear in public, in the diſguiſe of a mountebank, to be an eye-witneſs of a lady's beauty, of which he had heard only from report, and after eſcaping from the apprehended conſequences of this exorbitant frolic, which had brought him within the cenſure of a court of judicature, upon the bare declaration of the judges in his favour, and againſt thoſe he had cauſed to be unjuſtly accuſed; that he ſhould again aſſume another ſhape, that of an apparitor or tipſtaff; make a pretended will;

will; leave all his money, jewels, and effects, pretendedly to so wretched a fellow as a pimp and parasite; and all this with no other view than to mortify, insult, and abuse, those whom he had gulled, while yet the sentence of the court was depending, is a matter as absurd and improbable as any thing acted at the Italian comedy.

In the year 1731, the elder Mills acted Volpone; Wilks, Mosca; Colley Cibber, Corvino; Ben Jonson, Corbaccio; Mrs. Horton, Lady Would-be; and Celia by Mrs. Butler. About three years after, it was acted to still more advantage, for Quin excelled Mills in Volpone. In the Mountebank he assumed all the art, trick, and voluble impudence, of a charlatan; though W. Mills, who succeeded Wilks in Mosca, fell below his predecessor, yet his father, who submitted to play Corvino, was superior to C. Cibber in that part. Cibber seemed, I thought, to jest with the character. Mills was in earnest, and had a stronger voice to expreſs paſſionate and jealous rage than the other. Jonſon kept his old part, but Milward's Voltore was a fine copy of law oratory. Mrs. Clive, I need not ſay, gave infinite entertainment in Lady Wou'd-be. Though Celia is but a ſhort part, to Mrs. Butler's great commendation, ſhe rendered it extremely intereſting.

To omit mentioning the part of the firſt avocatori, or ſuperior judge, would be an act of injuſtice; for it was repreſented with great propriety by the venerable Mr. Boman, at that time verging to the eightieth year of his age. This actor was the laſt of the Bettertonian ſchool. By the remains of this man, the ſpectators might gueſs at the perfection to which the old maſters in acting had arrived. Boman pronounced the ſentence upon the ſeveral delinquents, in the comedy, with becoming gravity, grace, and dignity.

Mr. Garrick had long wiſhed to revive Volpone, and to act the principal character. The parts were tranſcribed and de-

livered

livered to the actors, but the acting of the play was superseded by some means not known.

The writers, upon dramatic poetry, of the last century, and during a considerable part of the present, have concurred in extolling the merits of the Silent Woman. Lowin, I think, originally acted Morose, and Taylor, Trewit. Mr. Dryden, in his Essay on dramatic Poetry, has given a very advantageous character of this play. After all the panegyric bestowed upon it, the play is of that number which needs much forgiveness, if it really has a title to much commendation. The great licentiousness of its dialogue was no obstacle to its success when originally performed; nor, in the reign of Charles II. when revived. But, as the age advanced in decency of manners, the less could the Silent Woman be tolerated. When it was revived, about thirty years since, under the management of Mr. Garrick, with perseverance it was dragged on for a few nights.

The managers acquired neither profit nor reputation by the exhibition of it. Some expreſſions met with ſevere marks of the ſpectators diſpleaſure. The character of Moroſe, upon whoſe peeviſh and perverſe humour the plot of the comedy depends, is that of a whimſical recluſe, whoſe diſpoſition can bear no ſound but that which he utters himſelf. If this were the whole of his character, he would ſtill be a good object for comic ſatire, but the melancholy of Moroſe degenerates into malice and cruelty. In extreme old age, to diſinherit a worthy young man, his nephew, he enters into the bonds of matrimony. The ſchemes therefore which are contrived to diſturb his repoſe and torment his mind, are proper medicines for ſuch a man, and juſtified by the ſtricteſt morality.

But, beſides the licentiouſneſs of the manners, and quaintneſs of expreſſion, in the Silent Woman, the frequent alluſions to forgotten cuſtoms and characters render it impoſſible to be ever revived with

any

any probability of ſucceſs. To underſtand Jonſon's comedies perfectly, we ſhould have before us a ſatirical hiſtory of the age in which he lived. I queſtion whether the diligence of Mr. Steevens and Mr. Malone could dig up a very complete explanation of this author's alluſions. Mr. Colman, after all the pains and ſkill he could beſtow on this comedy, found that it was labour loſt; there was no reviving the dead. The audience were as much diſguſted with Jonſon's old ruffs and bands, as the wits of James I. were with Hyeronimo's old cloak and the Spaniſh tragedy.

It muſt yet be confeſſed, that the gentlemen of this comedy, though perhaps too learned for the preſent day, converſe with an eaſy gaiety and liberal familiarity, ſuperior to any of this writer's productions. In the firſt act there is a ſonnet, which, for the vivacity and elegance of its turn of thought, I cannot forbear tranſcribing:

Still to be neat, ſtill to be dreſs'd
As you were going to a feaſt;
Still to be powder'd, ſtill perfum'd;
Lady, 'tis to be preſum'd,
Though art's hid cauſes are not found,
All is not ſweet, all is not ſound.
Give me a look, give me a face,
That makes ſimplicity a grace;
Robes looſely flowing, hair as free;
Such ſweet neglect more taketh me
Than all th'adulteries of art,
That ſtrike my eyes, but not my heart.

The author, agreeably to his old cuſtom, has made very free with the ancients: he has borrowed from Juvenal, Ovid de Arte Amandi, and Plautus's Aulularia.

We are told, that the Fox was conceived and brought forth in ſix weeks. But Jonſon's dramatic muſe lay fallow for four years; for Volpone was acted in 1605, and the Silent Woman not till the year 1609. Some new quarrel with the eſtabliſhed comedians, I ſuppoſe, cauſed him to have recourſe again to his children of the Revels, though

though he had loſt his favourite boy, Sal. Pavy, whoſe hiſtrionical abilities, and wonderful ſkill in repreſenting old men, though not arrived to his fourteenth year, he celebrated in a copy of verſes to his memory.

Such was the authority of Jonſon's name, that the king's comedians, eſtabliſhed at the Reſtoration, claiming a prior right of choice to the Duke of York's players, ſeized upon Ben Jonſon's three moſt eſteemed comedies and his two tragedies.

Cartwright, who was a bookſeller as well as an actor, played Moroſe. He is mentioned by name in the Rehearſal. —— Major Mohun was celebrated for True-Wit. The famous Lacy acted Captain Otter.

About fifty or ſixty years ſince, great reſpect was paid to this comedy; for Booth, Wilks, the elder Mills, and Colley Cibber, acted the Dauphin, Truewit, Clerimont, and Sir John Daw. Such an exhibition

exhibition of comic diſtreſs, in old Ben Jonſon's Moroſe, I have hardly ever ſeen in any other actor. He and Weſton are the only comedians I can remember, that, in all the parts they repreſented, abſolutely forgot themſelves. I have ſeen very great players, nay, ſuperior, in ſome reſpects, to them, at leaſt in the art of colouring and high finiſhing, when on the ſtage laugh at a blunder of a performer or ſome accidental impropriety of the ſcene: but theſe men were ſo truly abſorbed in character, that they never loſt ſight of it. Jonſon ſtayed on the ſtage to the laſt, till within about two years of eighty; but his very dregs were reſpectable. He died in 1742; and, a few months before his death, was out of humour, that the agent of the Dublin theatre, who came over on purpoſe to engage Mr. Garrick for the ſummer-months, had not made overtures to him. Otter was well acted by Shepherd, and Sir Amorous La Foole with vivacity by Theophilus Cibber.

The Alchemiſt was Ben Jonſon's laſt comedy of merit, for afterwards he produced

duced nothing very eſtimable. This play is, I think equal to any of this author's, in plot, character, and comic ſatire. The cataſtrophe is ſurely a bad one; a gentleman of fortune joining with his knaviſh ſervant, to cheat a parcel of bubbles of their money and goods, is equally mean and immoral. This play kept poſſeſſion of the ſtage long after the impoſture it was written to detect had ceaſed. It is worked up with amazing art; and, as its foundation is laid in avarice and impoſition, it affords a groupe of comic characters and variety of ſtage-buſineſs. However, it muſt be owned, that, for theſe laſt forty years, it has been ſupported by the action of a favourite Abel Drugger. Mr. Garrick freed the ſtage from the falſe ſpirit, ridiculous ſquinting, and vile grimace, which, in Theophilus Cibber, had captivated the public for ſeveral years, by introducing a more natural manner of diſplaying the abſurdities of a fooliſh tobacconiſt. At the ſame time, juſtice calls upon us to allow, that the ſimplicity of Weſton almoſt exceeded

ceeded the fine art of a Garrick, whose numberless excellences may spare a tribute of praise to this genuine child of nature. I cannot omit, in this place, to observe, that Mr. Garrick, by his own authority, intrenched upon the part of Kastril, acted incomparably by Mr. Yates, in the 4th act of the play; for the challenging of Surly, and driving him off the stage, belongs properly to the angry boy, and not to Abel, who, instead of being an auxiliary, took the field to himself. Colley Cibber I have seen act Subtle with great art; the elder Mills at the same time played Face with much shrewd spirit and ready impudence. The two Palmers have successively acted Face with much archness and solid characteristic bronze. Ben Griffin and Ben Jonson were much admired for their just representation of the canting puritanical preacher and his solemn deacon the botcher; there was an affected softness in the former which was finely contrasted by the fanatical fury of the other. —— Griffin's features seemed ready to be relaxed

laxed into a ſmile, while the ſtiff muſcles and fierce eye of the other admitted of no ſuppleneſs or compliance. There is ſtill to be ſeen a fine print of them in theſe characters, from a painting of Vanbleek: they are very ſtriking reſemblances of both comedians.

It has been ſaid, that Sir Epicure Mammon was drawn to imitate or outdo Falſtaff. I confeſs I ſee very little, if any, reſemblance. Sir Epicure is a fine portrait of a man learned in the art of luxury, gulled by his extreme rapacity and high reliſh for extravagant pleaſure.

I have never ſeen an adequate repreſenter of Sir Epicure, from Harper down to Love. The firſt ſeemed to have been taught by one who had juſter conceptions of what was to be done in the part than the player could execute. The outline was well drawn by Love; but there was a deficiency of glowing and warm tints which ſuch a rich dupe in folly required, and the character amply afforded. Love's conceptions of the part were juſt, but his want

of

of power to execute his meaning rendered his acting imperfect. The original actor of Sir Epicure, Lowin, was said to have represented it in a most perfect style of playing. Doll Common fell into Mrs. Clive's hands about fifty years ago. How she came afterwards into the possession of Mrs. Pritchard, while her friend was still in the company, I know not. If I remember rightly, the former, by lessening the vulgarity of the prostitute, did not give so just an idea of her as the latter. Mrs. Pritchard, by giving a full scope to her fancy as well as judgement, produced a complete resemblance of the practised and coarse harlot in Madam Doll.*

Macbeth.

---

* Dr. Johnson was the first who ventured to attack Jonson's infallibility in the following excellent lines:

Then Jonson came, instructed from the school,
To please in method and invent by rule.
His studious patience and laborious art,
By regular approach, assail'd the heart.
Cold approbation gave the lingering bayes,
For those who durst not censure, scarce could praise.
A mortal born, he met the general doom,
But left, like Eygpt's kings, a lasting tomb.

Macbeth.

CHAPTER XXVI.

Conjectures on the author's design in writing the tragedy of Macbeth.—Dr. Johnson's observations on witchcraft. — Shakspeare's use of vulgar errors.—Davenant's alteration of Macbeth. — Taste for rhyming plays in the reign of Charles II. — *Betterton obliged to submit to his superiors.—Defence of the modern stage-witches. — Waxen image of K. Duffus. — A curious poisoning girdle. — King James* I. *and Sir John Harrington. —Buchanan's dream.* — Studied in death *and* Safe towards your love and honour *explained. — Sickness, Thompson. — Crown of Scotland not hereditary. — Reason for Macbeth's treason. — Pity in the figure of a new born child. — Lady Macbeth and Clytemnestra. — Philip of Macedon compared*

pared to a ſponge. — Burbage. — Betterton. — Mills unequal to Macbeth. — Anecdote of a country gentleman. — Quin. — Moſſop. — Garrick. — Caſhel. — Anecdote of him and an inſidious rival.—Both died about the ſame time.

THE author had more than one thing in view when he wrote the tragedy of Macbeth. James I. loved the muſes; and, to his own and the poet's honour, diſtinguiſhed our Shakſpeare by particular marks of favour. His plays, we have the authority of Ben Jonſon to aver, gave the king great delight; and our beſt editors ſpeak of a letter which James wrote to him in his own hand: a very ſingular mark of royal favour, and an evident proof of the king's good taſte, humanity, and condeſcenſion.

To compliment his royal maſter as the deſcendant of Banquo, and the firſt of our monarchs,

'That twofold balls and treble ſceptres carry'd,'

was

was one main motive to the choice of the ſubject. James's belief in witchcraft, and his pretended knowledge of dæmonology, on which ſubject he publiſhed a volume, was, I believe, another inducement in order to gain his prince's favour. In an account Sir James Harrington has given of a long conference he had with James, he informs us that a conſiderable part of the king's diſcourſe turned upon witchcraft. I farther believe that there was another, and a political, reaſon which prevailed upon Shakſpeare to make a part of the Scottiſh hiſtory the ſubject of a play. The Engliſh and Scotch, united under one king, was a ſplendid novelty, as well as a matter of great conſequence to both. The perpetual wars, which had been carried on with great animoſity, for above five or ſix hundred years, between the inhabitants of the northern and ſouthern parts of the iſland, had contributed to embitter the ſpirits of both, and the ſudden eſtabliſhment of government under one prince could not im-

 mediately

mediately remove that diſpleaſure which had ſo long irritated them. Shakſpeare, therefore, choſe a ſubject which he thought would render the Scots important in their own eyes, and in the opinion of their new allies and fellow ſubjects. He has, beſides, very happily contrived to celebrate the humanity, courage, and generoſity, of his own countrymen, in the ſame piece. The lawful heir to the crown of Scotland is honourably maintained and ſupported, in the court of an Engliſh king, by the bravery of whoſe ſubjects the baniſhed prince is reſtored, and the uſurper defeated. This was a fair and honourable method of making court to both Engliſh and Scotch.

Dr. Johnſon's obſervations on witchcraft are learned and inſtructive: nothing can be added to them, at leaſt by me.

The impreſſions made on the mind of Shakſpeare, reſpecting witches, fairies, and inchantment, produced, in his riper years, ſuch amazing deſcriptions of the ſuppoſed powers, manners, and magic charms, of

theſe

theſe imaginary beings, as were wonderfully ſuited to the credulous age in which he lived. Like other great poets, he took advantage of the popular ſuperſtition to create ſuch phantoms of the imagination, which the weak and credulous believed as implicitly as the articles of their creed, while the more ſagacious conſidered them as efforts of fancy and effuſions of genius, which contributed to the main deſign of the poet,—to delight.

At the Reſtoration, few of our author's plays were written to the palate of the court and thoſe who aſſumed the direction of the public amuſements. After Macbeth had been thrown aſide, or neglected for ſome years, Sir William Davenant undertook to refine and reduce it, as near as poſſible, to the ſtandard of the taſte in vogue. He likewiſe brought it, as well as he could, to the reſemblance of an opera. In the muſical part he was aſſiſted by Mr. Locke, an eminent maſter of muſic. It muſt be confeſſed the ſongs of Hecate, and the other witches, have a ſolemn a-adaption to the beings for whom they were compoſed. Dances of furies were invented for the incantation-ſcene in the fourth act, and near fifty years ſince I ſaw our beſt dancers employed in the exhibition of infernal ſpirits. Had Davenant ſtopped here, it had been well for his reputation, but this ill-inſtructed admirer of Shakſpeare altered the plan of the author's deſign, and deſtroyed that peculiarity which diſtinguiſhes Macbeth from ſeveral of our author's pieces. The jingle of rhyme delighted the ears of our court critics, for no other reaſon, which I can diſcover, but becauſe the plays of the French nation, and eſpecially their tragedies, wore the chiming fetters; but the dramatic poets of France knew that their language was too weak for blank verſe, or for lines of twelve feet, without the aſſiſtance of rhyme, and therefore, what was mere neceſſity in them, the falſe judges of our language conſidered as an eſſential beauty.

In

In the Memoirs of Mr. Garrick I have quoted ſome part of a ſcene between Macbeth and his lady, upon the moſt ſerious and important ſubject, where poverty of ſentiment is only exceeded by wretchedneſs of rhyme. Davenant had, indeed, disfigured the whole piece, yet, notwithſtanding all his added deformities and ſad mutilations, ſo much of the original Macbeth was ſtill retained, that it continued, from the revival in 1665 to 1744, a very favourite entertainment of the ſtage. Betterton, who was then at the head of the duke of York's company, under Sir William Davenant, whatever his own taſte might be, was obliged to fall in with the views of his maſter and the faſhion of the times.

Happily for the lovers of Shakſpeare, Mr. Garrick, ſome years before he was a patentee, broke through the fetters of fooliſh cuſtom and arbitrary impoſition: he reſtored Macbeth to the public almoſt in the ſame dreſs it was left us in, by the author. A ſcene or two, which were not conducive to the action, he threw out in repreſentation; others that were too long he judiciouſly pruned; very few additions were made, except in ſome paſſages of the play neceſſary to the better explanation of the writer's intention. He compoſed, indeed, a pretty long ſpeech for Macbeth, when dying, which, though ſuitable perhaps to the character, was unlike Shakſpeare's manner, who was not prodigal of beſtowing abundance of matter on characters in that ſituation. But Garrick excelled in the expreſſion of convulſive throes and dying agonies, and would not loſe any opportunity that offered to ſhew his ſkill in that part of his profeſſion.

Act I. Scene I.

FIRST WITCH.

When ſhall we three meet again?

It has been an old complaint of ſtage critics, that the parts of the witches are always diſtributed amongſt the low comedians, who, by miſtaking the ſenſe of the author,

author, render thoſe ſentiments ridiculous which were deſigned by him to be ſpoken with gravity and ſolemnity. Should we ſuppoſe this charge to be well founded, it would not be a very eaſy taſk to remove it; for the tragedians are all employed in various parts of the drama, ſuited to their ſeveral abilities, ſo that none but the comic actors are left to wear gowns, beards, and coifs. But, I confeſs, I do not ſee the propriety of the accuſation. There is, in the witches, ſomething odd and peculiar, and approaching to what we call humour. The manners beſtowed on theſe beings are more ſuitable to our notions of comic than tragic action, and better fitted to Yates and Edwin than Henderſon and Smith. Nor do I ſee any impropriety in the manner adopted by the preſent comedians, who have too much underſtanding to ſacrifice ſentiment to grimace, or propriety to buffoonery. From the dramatis perſonæ of Davenant's Macbeth, we ſee the parts of the witches given to the low comedians of thoſe times, and in this the alterer, who had ſeen plays at the Globe, and in Blackfriers, long before the civil wars, followed, in all probability, the practice of the old ſtage,

WITCH.

Weary ſev'nnights nine times nine
Shall he dwindle, peak, and pine.

The Highlands of Scotland ſeem to have been the favourite reſort of witches and inchanters, where they are ſuppoſed to have performed their moſt powerful charms and diabolical incantations; and more particularly the town of Foris, near which place Macbeth was firſt accoſted by theſe beings. A waxen image of King Daffus, ſays Buchanan, was found roaſting at a fire, in that town, before ſome infernal hags, who were immediately ſeized and puniſhed; upon the deſtroying the image, the king, it is ſaid, recovered. Buchanan did not rely much on the truth of the ſtory, but gave it as it was related by former writers, though he could not find it authenticated

authenticated by ancient record. This ſtrange power, of weakening or killing the bodies of men at a diſtance, is of very ancient date. Lambard, in his Topographical Dictionary, mentions a curious girdle, which was ſo ſtrongly poiſoned as to kill a man at a conſiderable diſtance; it was intended, by a certain perſon or perſons, to diſpatch the Dean of York. The girdle was brought to Smithfield, as heretical, and there burnt.

WITCHES.

The *weïrd* ſiſters hand in hand.

To the learned notes of Dr. Warburton and Mr. Steevens, upon the word *weïrd*, I ſhall only add, that the gloſſariſt of Douglas's tranſlation of Virgil derives *weïrd* from the Anglo-Saxon *wyrd*, fatum, fortuna, eventus; *Wwyrde*, Fata, Parcæ. The old Scotch curſe, of 'waeworth him,' is apparently derived from *weïrd*, or *weyward*. Theſe weyward ſiſters ſeem to be akin to the Eumenides of the Greeks. The

Furies

Furies are prototypes of the northern Parcæ.

BANQUO.

——— What are theſe,
So wither'd, and ſo wild in their attire?

When James I. aſked Sir John Harrington, 'Why the devil did work more with ancient women than others?' Sir John replied, 'We were taught hereof in Scripture, *where it is told, that the devil walketh in dry places*.'

WITCH.

All hail, Macbeth! hail to thee, thane of Glamis!

In the relation of this part of the hiſtory, Buchanan differs entirely from Hollingſhead, who copied the tranſlator of Boetius. He relates, that, when he was at a diſtance from the court, Macbeth, on a certain night, dreamt that he ſaw three women, of an auguſt and more-than-human form, who ſaluted him by the ſeveral titles

titles of Angus and Murray, and, laſtly, of King.

MACBETH.

——— My dull brain was wrought
With things forgot.

'I was ruminating on matters not worth your hearing or my remembrance.'

Scene IV.

MALCOLM.

As one that had been ſtudy'd in his death.

'Studied in his death' is a phraſe borrowed from the theatre: to be ſtudied in a part is to have got it by rote, or to have made yourſelf maſter of it. Mr. Steevens hath, with great probability, ſuppoſed, that, in the deſcription of Cawdor's death, the author had a retroſpect to the behaviour of Eſſex at his execution. He was, by James himſelf, eſteemed to be one of his martyrs; and it is not improbable that Shakſpeare was perſonally acquainted with the dear and

and unfortunate friend of his patron, Southampton.

MACBETH.

Which do but what they ſhould, by doing every thing
Safe towards your love and honour.

The ſeveral propoſed emendations of this paſſage, by Mr. Theobald, Dr. Warburton, Dr. Johnſon, and Dr. Kenrick, are by no means ſatisfactory. Dr. Johnſon candidly doubts his alteration of *ſafe* to *ſhapes*; the *fiefs*, or *fief'd*, of Dr. Warburton, is not admiſſible; and Kenrick's *ward*, though the moſt plauſible, does not, I believe, come up to the intention of the author. I have before me a copy of Shakſpeare in folio, the ſecond edition, which formerly belonged to Mr. William Thompſon, of Queen's College, Oxford, author of a poem on Sickneſs: in the margin he puts a queſtion, whether it ſhould not be *life* and *honour* inſtead of *love* and *honour?* and this conjecture is ſubmitted to the reader, as at leaſt

leaſt preferable to any emendation as yet advanced.

MACBETH.

The Prince of Cumberland!—that is a ſtep
On which I muſt fall down, or elſe o'er-leap.

The mind of Macbeth had been greatly agitated by the preceding prophecies of the witches, and the completion of part of them. His fancy had preſented to his mind the accompliſhment of the whole, by an act, the thought of which alone had ſtruck him with reluctant horror. He ſeems to have reſembled Hazael, in the Scriptures, who, being told, by the prophet Eliſha, he ſhould bring terrible calamities upon the people of Iſrael, cried out, 'Is thy ſervant a dog, that he ſhould do theſe things?' But the poet artfully throws in freſh fuel to ſtimulate his ambition, by the King's nominating his ſon Prince of Cumberland. The crown of Scotland was not, as Mr. Steevens has obſerved, hereditary; and every reader of Scottiſh

Scottifh hiftory will be convinced, that prudence and neceffity both co-operated to prevent a regular fucceffion of the fon to the father in that kingdom. The kings of Scotland were fo often immaturely deftroyed, by foreign wars, factious nobility, or private treachery, that it was wifely ordered the crown fhould devolve on the next of kin arrived to maturity of age and ripenefs of underftanding, and not to the fon of the deceafed monarch under age. This was the practice in that kingdom for many ages. Duncan, by appointing his fon, then a minor,* Prince of Cumberland, a dignity like that of Prince of Wales with us, cut off all Macbeth's hopes of gaining the crown in cafe the King fhould have died before Malcolm arrived to years of maturity. Buchanan fays expreflly, that, by this action, Duncan had given him fufficient caufe of difcontent.

Scene

* Vixdum puberem. Buchan. Hift. lib. 7.

Scene VII.

MACBETH.

——— But, in theſe caſes,
We ſtill have judgement here, that we but teach
Bloody inſtructions.

The beſt comment on this paſſage is to be read in the preface to Sir Walter Raleigh's Hiſtory of the World, and more particularly in the following quotation from it: 'For thoſe kings, which have ſold the blood of others at a low rate, have but made a market for their own enemies to buy of theirs at the ſame price.'

MACBETH.

——— Beſides, this Duncan
Hath borne his faculties ſo meek, hath been
So clear in his great office ———

The only fault, attributed by hiſtorians to the unhappy Duncan, was exceſs of humanity and gentleneſs of diſpoſition. — 'Vir ſumma humanitate,' ſays Buchanan, 'ac majore erga ſuos indulgentia quam in rege par erat.'

IDEM.

IDEM.

And Pity, like a naked new-born babe
Striding the blaſt, or heaven's cherubin hors'd
Upon the ſightleſs couriers of the air,
Shall blow the horrid deed in ev'ry eye,
That tears ſhall drown the wind.

The author, not ſatisfied with preſenting us with that tender and beautiful image of pity, a new-born babe, riſes to the more ſublime idea of an angel mounted on the wings of the wind, to communicate the diſaſtrous news of a monarch's murder to the world. The thought ſeems to have been borrowed from the eighteenth pſalm: ' He rode upon the cherubim and did fly; he came flying upon the wings of the wind!'

Fenton, in his tragedy of Mariamne, in the following lines of Sohemus to Salome, makes Pity young and ſhort-lived:

——— In diſtant ages paſt,
Pity dy'd young, of grief, they ſay, to ſee
An eagle wreak his malice on a wren.

LADY MACBETH.

——— Was the hope drunk
Wherein you dreſs'd yourſelf?

In other words, ‘ Were you ſober when you firſt entertained the conception of killing the king?’

The undaunted ſpirit and determinedly-wicked reſolution of Macbeth's wife are no where to be matched, in any female character of the ancient Greek drama, except in the Clytemneſtra of Æſchylus. Their ſituations are different, but their characters bear a great reſemblance. Both are haughty and intrepid, artful and cruel, in the extreme: Clytemneſtra plans the murder of Agamemnon, her huſband, and is herſelf the aſſaſſin; Lady Macbeth not only encourages her huſband to kill the King, but enjoys the fact when it is done; the remorſe of the murderer ſhe conſiders as puſillanimity, and helps to remove the appearance of guilt from him by ſmearing the faces of the ſleeping grooms.

LADY MACBETH.

——— What not put upon
His *ſpongy* officers?

Men drenched in liquor are with great propriety compared to *ſponges*. When Æſchines praiſed Philip King of Macedon for his abilities in drinking, Demoſthenes told him, 'that was a commendation fit for a *ſponge*.'

Of the original actors in Macbeth we can form no judgement; for nothing is to be found relating to them in books, nor has tradition handed down any thing concerning them. We may indeed conjecture, that Burbage, who exhibited Richard III. was, by the author, ſelected to repreſent Macbeth. Not only becauſe he was the firſt tragedian of the times, but, from his performing characters of a ſimilar caſt, we may ſuppoſe him to have been better adapted to it than Taylor, (another eminent actor in tragedy,) or any player of that age.

The

The Tatler has celebrated Betterton for his excellence in Macbeth as well as other principal tragic parts. Cibber has not particularly diſtinguiſhed this great comedian for his performance of this character; that he acted it to the very verge of his life, I learned in a converſation with Mr. Ryan. Though Booth was one of the company of comedians who obtained a licence in the year 1711, ſoon after the death of Betterton, Wilks, with great partiality, gave Macbeth to Mr. John Mills, a player whom he patroniſed. But Mills was deficient in genius to diſplay the various paſſions and turbulent ſcenes of the character. Mills was, in perſon, inclined to the athletic ſize; his features large, though not expreſſive; his voice was manly and powerful, but not flexible; his action and deportment decent. In voice and perſon he was not very unlike Mr. Edward Berry, whom Colley Cibber uſed to term a ſecond old Mills. I have ſeen him in Macbeth; but neither his manner of ſpeaking, his action, nor his deportment, made any impreſſion on my mind greatly to his advantage. He ſpoke, indeed, the celebrated ſoliloquy on the progreſs of time, beginning with 'Tomorrow! tomorrow! and tomorrow!' with propriety and feeling, and it produced conſiderable effect on the audience.

It was a matter of concern, to judges of theatrical merit, to ſee ſuch actors as Booth and Powell condemned to repreſent the inferior parts of Banquo and Lenox, when Mills was ſo improperly ſet over their heads. Roberts the player, author of a letter to Mr. Pope concerning ſome paſſages in his preface to Shakſpeare, told me that the indignation of a country gentleman broke out one night, during the acting of this play, in a very odd manner. The 'ſquire, after having been heartily tired with Mills, on the appearance of his old companion, George Powell, in the fourth act, cried out, loud enough to be heard by the audience, 'For God's ſake, George, give me a ſpeech and let me go home.'

Quin's

Quin's figure and countenance, in this character, ſpoke much in his favour; but he was deficient in animated utterance, and wanted flexibility of tone. He could neither aſſume the ſtrong agitation of mind before the murder of the king, nor the remorſe and anguiſh in conſequence of it:—much leſs could he put on that mixture of deſpair, rage, and frenzy, that mark the laſt ſcenes of Macbeth. During the whole repreſentation he ſcarce ever deviated from a dull, heavy, monotony.

Moſſop's power of expreſſion, in ſeveral ſituations of Macbeth, commanded attention and applauſe. Had he been acquainted with variety of action and eaſy deportment, he would have been juſtly admired in it. Barry ought never to have attempted that which was ſo oppoſite to his natural manner. He was not formed to repreſent the terrible agonies of Macbeth.

The genius of a Garrick could alone comprehend and execute the complicated paſſions of this character. From the firſt

 ſcene,

ſcene, in which he was accoſted by the witches to the end of the part, he was animated and conſiſtent. The tumult raiſed in his mind, by the prophecy of the witches, was expreſſed by feelings ſuitable to the occaſion, nor did he ſuffer the marks of this agitation to be entirely diſſipated in the preſence of Duncan, which he diſcovered to the audience in no obſcure manner; more eſpecially when the king named Malcolm prince of Cumberland.

Before I conclude my account of the ſeveral actors who perſonated Macbeth, I muſt take notice of a piece of ſtage perfidy which had like to have produced diſagreeable conſequences to a performer of that character.

Oliver Caſhel was by birth an Iriſhman, well educated, and of a good family. His inclination to the profeſſion of acting brought him firſt to the ſtage of Drury-lane, and afterwards to that of Covent-Garden, where he met with ſuch encouragement from Mr. Rich, that he excited the jealouſy jealoufy of an actor who had been for a confiderable time advancing equally in the favour of the manager. Cafhel was bred in high tory principles, which he took no pains to conceal, but indifcreetly threw out his notions of government and political affairs in mixed companies. The man was innocent of any intention to difturb the ftate; he was only rafh in the ufe of expreffions which might be interpreted to his difadvantage. The nation was, in 1746, involved in a French and Spanifh war, and a rebellion had broken out in Scotland. The rival of Cafhel, though not known by him to be fuch, took advantage of his unguarded warmth of temper, and fecretly laid an information againft him at the fecretary of ftate's office. The accufed perfon was taken up by a general warrant, and examined by the fecretary of ftate. Nothing worthy the notice of government appearing in his diffavour, he was fet at liberty. The firft place he reforted to was the Bedford Coffee-houfe, fee-houſe, where he found his ſecret and perfidious enemy waiting the iſſue of his information. Caſhel was going very innocently to relate his unexpected adventure to him; but the other, ſhocked at his ſight, ran out of the coffee-houſe in great haſte, to ſhun the man whom he had ſo baſely endeavoured to injure. Soon after this tranſaction, news arrived from Scotland of the battle at Falkirk, where, it was ſuppoſed, the rebels had gained ſome ſlight advantage. The king was adviſed to go to the theatre and to command the tragedy of Macbeth. Caſhel's examination before a miniſter of ſtate was known to the public, and Rich doubted whether it would be prudent to permit him to act the principal character before the king. Quin heard of the manager's ſcruples, and offered his ſervice without any expectation of reward. But the king being aſked if he had any objection to Mr. Caſhel's acting before him, anſwered, " By no means, he would be altogether as acceptable as any

any other player." A few months after, Cashel was seized with an apoplectic fit, as he was acting on the stage at Norwich, which he did not long survive; his enemy died, I believe, much about the same time.

CHAPTER XXVII.

Banquo's deſcription of Duncan's complacency. — Macbeth's drink. — The meaning of the word wines. — *Dagger-ſcene. — Duke of Parma and David Garrick. — Quotation from Æſchylus. — Tarquin's ſtrides. — Connoiſeur and Garrick. — Lady Macbeth works herſelf to the encouragement of murder. — By what methods. —* Say their prayers, and moſt need of bleſſing, *explained. — Quotation from the hymns of Orpheus and the Choœphoræ of Æſchylus. — The play of Macbeth an admirable ſermon againſt murder. — Excellence of Garrick and Pritchard.—Short hoſe of the French.—Story of Nokes.—Mrs. Porter.—Direction to the actor of Macduff.*—Unmannerly *explained. —* Breech'd, *from Maſſinger. —* Naked faculties, *note upon. — Loud grief to be ſuppreſſed. — Behaviour of the actors in in a ſcene after the king's murder. — King Duffus. — Donald and his wife. — Perfect ſpy of the time. — Lady Macbeth's diſcontent. — Melancholy ſtate of the murderer. —* Deareſt chuck *explained. — Feaſt ſold. — Ghoſt of Banquo. — Lloyd's verſes. — Garrick's opinion of the merit of Macbeth. — Garrick and Mrs. Pritchard. — Their various excellences. — Quotation from Æſchylus. — Young in deed. — Pit of Acheron and the brook of Acheneen. — Macbeth and Macduff's mutual jealouſy from Buchanan.*

BANQUO.

——————And ſhut up
In meaſureleſs contentment.

BANQUO's deſcription of Duncan's full enjoyment of his entertainment preſents a moſt amiable picture of a benevolent mind. The words *meaſureleſs contentment* give an idea of unbounded goodneſs and complacency.

MACBETH.

MACBETH.

Go bid thy miſtreſs, when my drink is ready, ſhe ſtrike upon the bell.

In the times of the feudal ſyſtem, kings, princes, barons, and all perſons of diſtinguiſhed birth and rank, before they went to reſt, partook of a collation called the *wines*, conſiſting of delicate cates and wine, warmed and mixed with certain ſpices. Froiſſart eſteemed it a great piece of good fortune that he ſpent the greateſt part of his life in the courts of princes, for thereby he had gained *an opportunity of drinking the wines, which*, he ſays, *contributed much to his comfort and repaſt.** This is the cordial which we may reaſonably ſuppoſe Shakſpeare meant by the drink.

IDEM.

Is this a dagger which I ſee before me!

Many ſtage critics ſuppoſe this to be one of the moſt difficult ſituations in acting. The ſudden ſtart on ſeeing the dagger in

* Froiſſart. Tom. ii. Chap. 81.

in the air,—the endeavour of the actor to ſeize it,—the diſappointment,—the ſuggeſtion of its being only a viſion of the diſturbed fancy,—the ſeeing it ſtill in form moſt palpable, with the reaſoning upon it,——theſe are difficulties which the mind of Garrick was capable of encountering and ſubduing. So happy did he think himſelf in the exhibition of this ſcene, that, when he was in Italy, and requeſted by the duke of Parma to give a proof of his ſkill in action, to the admiration of that prince, he at once threw himſelf into the attitude of Macbeth's ſeeing the air-drawn dagger. The duke deſired no farther proof of Garrick's great excellence in his profeſſion, being perfectly convinced, by this ſpecimen, that he was an abſolute maſter of it.

IDEM.

——— Now o'er one half the world
Nature lies dead, and wicked dreams abuſe
The curtain'd ſleep.

This is not unlike a paſſage in the Coœphoræ of Æſchylus:

For,

For, in the ſtill and midnight hour,
When darkneſs aids his hideous power,
Affright, that breathes his vengeance deep,
Haunts with wild dreams the curtain'd ſleep.

POTTER'S ÆSCHYLUS.

IDEM.

With Tarquin's raviſhing *ſtrides.*

Mr. Steevens has, from Spencer and Harrington's Arioſto, brought inſtances to prove that the word *ſtride* does not always convey the idea of violent motion. Notwithſtanding this, I believe that almoſt every body, who reads the line as above quoted, will ſuppoſe the word to import ſomething like tumult and noiſe. But all diſputes, about the word *ſtrides*, may eaſily be determined by reſtoring what, I think, is the genuine reading, *ſides*, which was firſt removed by Mr. Pope, who, in its ſtead, ſubſtituted *ſtrides*. 'I am now, ſays Macbeth, moving towards my purpoſe with the cautious ſteps of the raviſhing Tarquin, or the ſilent pace of a ghoſt.' The ſides of a man, in our language, like the

the latera or humeri of the Latins, signify his power and ability.

In Twelfth Night, the duke tells Viola,

> ——There is *no woman's sides*
> Can bide the beating of so strong a passion
> As love doth give my heart.

By a very common figure, the sides of a man stand for the man himself.

IDEM.

> ——Hear it not, Duncan, for it is a bell
> That summons thee to heaven or to hell!

The thought is solemn, though, I believe, every reader wishes there had been no chime on an occasion so tremendous. But Davenant lessens the gloom of the idea still farther, by an alteration very improper:

> ——Hear it not, Duncan, for it is a bell
> That rings my coronation and thy knell!

Upon Macbeth's going off the stage to perpetrate the murder, the author of the Connoiseur observes, that the actor's feelings must have been disturbed by his wi-

ping

ping the paint from his face to look more ghaſtly on his re-entrance, beſides the diſordering of his wig to give the appearance of buſtle and diſtraction. Would not the ſame author, if the actor had returned from the ſuppoſed murder as unruffled in dreſs and as florid in look as before, have juſtly remarked that he had forgotten the ſituation in which his author had placed him, for he bore no outward ſigns of a man concerned in the buſineſs of aſſaſſination? He might as well, too, have remarked that the player muſt have employed ſome of his time in dipping the ſtage-daggers in blood. But there is no end of ſuch criticiſm; I am only ſorry that remarks of this kind ſhould eſcape a writer not more remarkable for candour of ſpirit than force of genius.

LADY MACBETH.

That, which hath made them drunk, hath made me bold!
What hath quench'd them, hath given me fire!

By theſe lines being put in the mouth of Lady Macbeth, Shakſpeare ſeems unwilling to to ſuppoſe that one of the tender ſex could be wrought up to become an aſſociate in murder, without ſome preparation for it, by a degree of intoxication.

MACBETH.

But they did ſay their pray'rs, and addreſs'd them
Again to ſleep.

By 'ſaying their prayers,' the author means, they poured out ſuch ſhort addreſſes to the divine Being as men diſturbed by troubleſome dreams, or frightened by ſudden apprehenſion of danger, generally ejaculate: ſuch as imploring heaven's protection, begging forgiveneſs of ſins, and the like. This will give us the true meaning of what Macbeth ſays immediately after.

MACBETH.

———— I could not ſay amen,
When they did cry, Heav'n bleſs us! ——
I had moſt need of bleſſing.

Macbeth could not, even in his then diſtracted ſtate of mind, ſuppoſe that heaven would ſanctify murder by giving a bleſſing to the

 murderer.

murderer. Bleſſing is here put for pardon: ‘ I had moſt need of forgiveneſs.’

IDEM.

Macbeth doth murder ſleep !—the innocent ſleep !—
Sleep, that knits up the ravell'd ſleeve of care,
The death of each day's life, ſore labour's bath,
Balm of hurt minds, great nature's ſecond courſe,
Chief nouriſher in life's feaſt !———

Theſe attributes of ſleep greatly reſemble ſome beautiful lines in the Hymns of Orpheus to Night and Sleep:

Κλυθι, μακαιρα θεα, ——
Ευφροσυνε τερπνη, φιλοπαννυχε, μητερ ονειρων,
Ληθομεριμν' αγαθη τε, πονων αναπαυσιν εχουσα,——
Νυν τε μακαιρα Νυξ πολυολβιε, πασι ποθεινε, &c.

Ὑπνε, αναξ μακαρων παντων θνητων τ' ανθρωπων,——
Σωματα δεσμευων εν αχαλκευτοισι πεδησι,
Λυσιμεριμνε, κοπων ηδειαν εχων αναπαυσιν,
Και πασης λυπης ιερον παραμυθιον ερδων.

IDEM.

IDEM.

Will all great Neptune's ocean waſh this blood
Clean from my hand? No, this my hand will rather
The multitudinous ſea incarnadine!

The Chorus, in the Coœphoræ of Æſchylus, breathes ſentiments not unlike this of Macbeth:

——— Were all the ſtreams, that wind
Their mazy progreſs to the main,
To cleanſe this odious ſtain, in one combin'd,
The ſtreams combin'd would flow in vain.

Potter's Æſchylus.

IDEM.

To know my deed 'twere beſt not know myſelf.

'Whilſt I am conſcious of having committed this murder, I cannot but be miſerable; I have no remedy but in the total forgetfulneſs of the deed, or, to ſpeak more plainly, in the loſs of my ſenſes.'

The merit of this ſcene tranſcends all panegyric. Amongſt the many diſcourſes, which, from the earlieſt time to the preſent hour, have been compoſed on the ſubject of murder, it will be difficult to find ſo powerful a diſſuaſive or dehortation from that dreadful crime as the tragedy of Macbeth exhibits. In drawing the principal character of the play, the author has deviated ſomewhat from hiſtory; but, by abating the fierceneſs of Macbeth's diſpoſition, he has rendered him a fitter ſubject for the drama. The rational and ſevere delight, which the ſpectator feels from the repreſentation of this piece, proceeds, in a great meaſure, from the ſenſibility of the murderer, from his remorſe and agonies, and from the torments he ſuffers in the midſt of his ſucceſsful villany.

The repreſentation of this terrible part of the play, by Garrick and Mrs. Pritchard, can no more be deſcribed than I believe it can be equalled. I will not ſeparate theſe performers, for the merits of both were tranſcendent. His diſtraction of mind and agonizing horrors were finely contraſted by her ſeeming apathy, tranquillity, and confidence. The beginning of the ſcene after the

the murder was conducted in terrifying whispers. Their looks and action supplied the place of words. You heard what they spoke, but you learned more from the agitation of mind displayed in their action and deportment. The poet here gives only an outline to the consummate actor.— *I have done the deed! — Didst thou not hear a noise? — When? — Did you not speak?* — The dark colouring, given by the actor to these abrupt speeches, makes the scene awful and tremendous to the auditors! The wonderful expression of heartful horror, which Garrick felt when he shewed his bloody hands, can only be conceived and described by those who saw him! The expression of 'sorry sight!' is certainly not happy now. Words, which were highly expressive and energetic above one hundred and fifty years since, have, by length of time, lost their importance. —— Davenant, fifty years after, altered *sorry* to *dismal*; but perhaps a better word than that might still be substituted.

PORTER.

Who's there? — Here's an Engliſh tailor, come hither for ſtealing out of a French hoſe.

The archneſs of the joke, ſays Dr. Warburton, conſiſts in the French hoſe being very ſhort and ſtrait, for that tailor muſt be maſter of his trade who could ſteal any thing thence. Mr. Steevens declares freely, that Dr. Warburton made this objection at random, and quotes an old pamphlet of Stubbs to prove, 'the Gallick hoſen are made very large and wide, reaching down to their knees.' Dr. Farmer, in favour of Dr. Warburton, obſerves, that Mr. Steevens had forgotten the uncertainty of French faſhions, and quotes from an old book a paſſage to prove that French hoſe anſwered in length to their ſhort-ſkirted doublets. As a farther proof that our neighbours, the French, in the reign of Louis IV. were fond of ſhort doublets, I ſhall preſent the reader with a ſtage-anecdote from honeſt Downs, the theatrical hiſtorian, who relates,

relates, ‘ That, when King Charles II. and all his court, met his ſiſter, the Ducheſs of Orleans, at Dover, the comedy of Sir Solomon Single, acted before both courts, pleaſed her grace and all the ſpectators extremely. The French wore, at the ſame time, ſhort laced coats, ſome ſcarlet, ſome blue, adorned with broad waiſt-belts. Nokes had on, in the part of Sir Arthur Addle, one ſhorter than the reſt; the Duke of Monmouth gave him his ſword and belt from his ſide, and buckled it on himſelf, on purpoſe to mimic the French. Nokes looked more like a dreſſed-up ape than a man; ſo that, on his firſt entrance upon the ſtage, he put the king and the whole court into an exceſſive fit of laughter; at which, the French were very chagrined to ſee themſelves aped by ſuch a fool as Sir Arthur. Mr. Nokes kept the duke's ſword to his dying day.’

MACDUFF.

——— Up, up, and ſee
The great doom's image!

'A picture of horror not to be parallelled but in the univerſal ruin of the world at the laſt day.'

LADY MACBETH.

What's the buſineſs?

The players have long ſince removed Lady Macbeth from this ſcene. A London audience we may ſuppoſe not to be ſo critical as that of Athens, or ſuch an one as Oxford or Cambridge could ſupply. —— Many years ſince, I have been informed, an experiment was hazarded, whether the ſpectators would bear Lady Macbeth's ſurprize and fainting; but, however characteriſtical ſuch behaviour might be, perſons of a certain claſs were ſo merry upon the occaſion, that it was not thought proper to venture the Lady's appearance any more. Mr. Garrick thought, that even ſo favourite an actreſs as Mrs. Pritchard would not, in that ſituation, eſcape deriſion from the gentlemen in the upper regions. Mr. Macklin

Macklin is of opinion, that Mrs. Porter alone could have credit with an audience, to induce them to endure the hypocriſy of Lady Macbeth.

MACBETH.

O, yet I do repent me of my fury,
That I did kill them.

MACDUFF.

———— Why did you ſo?

The murder of Duncan's chamber-grooms, by Macbeth, juſtly raiſes ſuſpicion in Macduff. I have ſeldom ſeen an actor of this character, who rightly underſtood his ſituation: his eye ought to purſue and examine Macbeth's demeanour during the remainder of the ſcene, though not in ſuch a manner as to diſcover what paſſed in his mind to the ſuſpected perſon.

MACBETH.

Unmannerly breech'd with gore.

Propriety of expreſſion was not the principal ſtudy of Shakſpeare. He frequently lays

lays hold of the firſt word that meets his fancy; though I ſee no reaſon to cavil with *unmannerly*, which Mr. Warton ſupports very forcibly. The word, with compounds of the ſame import, are in good authors to be found in a ſenſe not very remote from this in Shakſpeare. In Dryden, *unmannered* ſignifies uncivil, rude, and brutal; *unmannerlineſs*, in Locke, is indecent behaviour and breach of civility. *Unmannerly*, in this quotation, means indecently in the higheſt degree! brutally! ſhockingly! ——— The propriety of the word *unmannerly*, in this place, may be juſtified by a like freedom taken by Greek and Latin authors in words ſeemingly as remote from their original meaning:—Dr. Clarke in a learned note upon Αλγησας δ'αχρειον ιδων, in the ſecond book of Homer's Iliad, l. 279, obſerves, that αχρειον ιδων elegantiſſime dictum eſt, et tam ſignificanter ut nil poſſit ſupra. Latine dicens *inutile tuens*, ſicuti *torvum tuens*, &c. Obſervandum autem αχρειος apud Græcos, quum de homine malo

malo dicitur, non utique eum exhibere qui ſimpliciter ſit *non utilis*, ſed qui ſit *maxime nequam*. Similiter apud optimos linguæ Romanæ auctores, inutile legitur id, non quod non utile modo, *ſed quicquid utili maxime eſt contrarium*. The whole note I would recommend to the peruſal of the candid and judicious reader.

Dr. Warburton's *reech'd*, inſtead of *breech'd*, is plauſible; but the old reading is well juſtified by Mr. Steevens, and ſtill more forcibly by Dr. Farmer. *Breech'd* was certainly a common word, in our author's time, applied to the covering of any thing, as well as a part of a man's body. Sometimes it ſignifies the direct contrary, as in Maſſinger's Guardian, act I. Durazzo, ſpeaking of his nephew's diſtant and baſhful courtſhip of his miſtreſs:

How he looks like a ſchool-boy that had play'd
The truant, and went to be *breech'd*.

BANQUO.

BANQUO.

And, when we have our naked faculties hid,
Which ſuffer in expoſure ———

In ſuch a cloud of words, Mr. Steevens is afraid leſt the meaning ſhould eſcape the reader; and therefore he informs them, that they are to underſtand by them, —— '*When we have clothed our half-dreſſed bodies, which may take cold from being expoſed to the air.*' Shakſpeare underſtood not only the propriety and decorum of the ſtage, but the genius of his audience, and would never ſend on his characters half-dreſſed. Such a ludicrous ſight, which no ſkill could prevent, would have excited loud burſts of laughter. This appearance certainly would be very natural; for the ringing of a bell, and a loud outcry of murder, muſt, in a palace, or any houſe, have drawn together the higheſt and loweſt of its inmates, ſome armed with one weapon, ſome with another: but, at ſuch a motley ſight, ſurely,

To be grave exceeds all power of face.

In

In the more advanced ſtate of the ſtage, Mr. Garrick would not riſk the appearance of half, or even diſordered, dreſs, though extremely proper, and what the incident of the fable and ſituation of the characters ſeemed to require. But the words will, I think, very eaſily bear another meaning: 'When we have recovered ourſelves from that grief and thoſe tranſports of paſſion, which, though juſtifiable from natural feeling and the ſad occaſion, do but expoſe the frailty and imbecility of our nature.'

Extreme grief and loud lamentations, however natural, and to be indulged in private, are ſurely not graceful in public, and are always there endeavoured to be ſuppreſſed. Our Shakſpeare is very careful to reſtrain exceſſive grief in the preſence of others. In Julius Cæſar, act III. the ſervant of Octavius, on ſeeing the dead body of Cæſar, cries 'O Cæſar!' and burſts into tears: Mark Antony checks his ſorrow, in that place, by ſaying, 'Thy heart is full; *get thee apart and weep*.' And Kent, in King Lear,

Lear, act IV. describing Cordelia's behaviour, when told of the cruelty of her sisters to her father:

——— Then she shook
The holy water from her heav'nly eyes,
And clamour moisten'd her.—Then away she started,
To deal with grief alone.

MACBETH.

Let's briefly put on manly readiness,
And meet in the hall together.

This scene of strong perturbation and deep sorrow requires, in the representation, the nicest and most accurate management. — The guilty Macbeth, though struggling to assume the appearance of innocence and deep concern, dares not meet the eye of any person. The rest walk up and down as if sighing and lamenting; only Macduff and the sons of Duncan seem, by their looks, to point out the murderer.

ROSS.

——— By the clock 'tis day,
And yet dark night strangles the travelling lamp.—

— Darkness

— Darkneſs doth the face of earth entomb,
When living light ſhould kiſs it.

From the hiſtory of King Duffus's murder, by Donald, governor of the citadel of Foris, Shakſpeare has borrowed ſome incidents and ſome embelliſhments for his fable. Duffus, having determined to bring to juſtice ſome robbers, who had laid waſte Murray, Roſs, and Caithneſs, cauſed them to be ſeized and brought to Foris, there to receive condign puniſhment. Donald was greatly offended that the king would not be prevailed upon to pardon ſome friends of his aſſociated in the robberies. His wife, who, in violence of diſpoſition, greatly reſembles Lady Macbeth, ſtimulated her huſband to murder the king from the conveniency of doing it; for, having the command of the caſtle, ſhe told him, he had the power of executing the deſign in his own hands. This, I take it, is Shakſpeare's *time and place agreeing*. Mr. Steevens has already produced the tale of the hawk and the mouſing owl from

from the ſame ſource with the killing of Duffus's grooms.*

The deſcription of darkneſs obſcuring the hemiſphere, by Roſs, is borrowed from the ſame hiſtory. Buchanan ſays, indeed, there was a general darkneſs, over all Scotland, after the murder of Duffus, that neither ſun nor moon were to be ſeen for the ſpace of ſix months after.

Act III. Scene I.

MACBETH.

Acquaint you with the *perfect ſpy* of the time.

Dr. Johnſon thinks, by the *perfect ſpy* is meant the third Murderer, whom Macbeth ſends to join the other two. But one of the two firſt who were employed did not ſo underſtand it, by queſtioning the third. ' The

* Something, ſimilar to this ſtory of the hawk and mouſing owl, we read in the Perſæ of Æſchylus.

ALOSSA. — An eagle I beheld
Fly to the altar of the ſun : — aghaſt
I ſtood, my friends, and ſpeechleſs ; when a hawk
With eager ſpeed runs thither, furious cuffs
The eagle with his wings, and with his talons
Unplumes his head : mean time th'imperial bird
Cow'rs to the blows, defenceleſs.—Potter's Æſchylus.

'The perfect ſpy of the time' is well explained by the words which follow, 'the moment of it,' that is, the very inſtant you are to begin your bloody buſineſs. At the ſame time the King diſmiſſes them, commanding them to ſtay within till he calls them. The ſending a third murdering aſſiſtant is an after-thought, proceeding from Macbeth's anxious impatience to have the buſineſs finiſhed.

LADY MACBETH.

——— Nought's had, all's ſpent,
Where our deſire is got without content.
'Tis ſafer to be that which we deſtroy,
Than, by deſtruction, dwell in doubtful joy.

The Lady is willing to enjoy the fruits of the abominable crime which her huſband, by her inſtigation and aſſiſtance, had committed; but, ſeeing diſcontent lay hold of his mind, and all their hopes of happineſs abortive, ſhe now begins to think it would be ſafer, that is, in our author's intention, *more eligible*, to be the

 murdered

murdered than the murderer. She was approaching to that ſtate of mind which is ſo beautifully deſcribed in the Tempeſt, where the good Gonſalvo, ſpeaking of Alonzo and his guilty aſſociates, ſays,

——— Their great guilt,
Like poiſon giv'n to work a great time after,
Now 'gins to bite their ſpirits.

LADY MACBETH.

——— Why do you keep alone,
Of *ſorrieſt fancies* your companions making?

'Sorrieſt fancies' do not here, as Dr. Johnſon imagines, ſignify worthleſs, ignoble, and vile, imaginations; but, doubtleſs, black, gloomy, and melancholy, reflections. Mr. Steevens admits, that *ſorrieſt* may poſſibly mean melancholy and diſmal, and quotes a paſſage from the Comedy of Errors to prove it; but he needed not have gone ſo far; as Macbeth, after committing the murder on Duncan, makes uſe of the word *ſorry* in that ſenſe: for, ſhewing his hands, in an agony he cries

cries out, 'This is a *sorry* sight!' this is a sight not to be viewed without horror!

MACBETH.

——— Unsafe the while that we
Must lave our honours in these flattering streams,
And make our faces vizards to our hearts.

Happy it is for the world, that the villain can seldom quietly and peaceably enjoy the fruits of his iniquity. He, who before found dissimulation and flattery his best conductors to the throne, is now surfeited with, and lothes, them. But *safer* signifies here, as in the preceding soliloquy of the Lady, *preferable*. He intends, by the word *unsafe*, likewise to express the disagreeable tenure by which he holds his life and crown, by being obliged to soothe and flatter those whom he mortally hates.

IDEM.

Be innocent of the knowledge, dearest *chuck*.

Chuck, from *chick*, or *chicken*; or perhaps a word of fondness borrowed from the

hen,

hen, who invites her little brood to partake of what ſhe has ſcratched from the ground, and emits a ſound reſembling *chuck* or *cluck*. Othello, act III. makes uſe of the ſame term:

What promiſe, *chuck*?

Scene IV. Banquet.

LADY MACBETH.

——— The feaſt is ſold
That is not often vouch'd while it is making.

'If you do not give due welcome to your gueſts, by paying them proper attention, the feaſt will reſemble a dinner at an inn, or ordinary, where every man pays for his ſhare of the entertainment.'

The ghoſt of Banquo riſes, and ſits in Macbeth's chair.

It has been queſtioned, whether Banquo's ghoſt ſhould not preſent itſelf to the imagination of Macbeth, as the dagger did before the murder of the King. The appearance of a ghoſt is thought by ſome a

mere

mere trick, a *jeu du théâtre*; and Lloyd, in his excellent poem of the Actor, has ridiculed, in very animated lines, the mealy appearance of Banquo:

When chilling horrors ſhake th'affrighted King,
And guilt torments him with her ſcorpion-ſting;
When keeneſt feelings at his boſom pull,
And fancy tells him that the ſeat is full;
Why need the ghoſt uſurp the monarch's place,
To frighten children with his mealy face?
The King alone ſhould form the phantom there,
And talk and tremble at the empty chair.

It muſt be confeſſed, theſe viſionary appearances are but helps to the unaccompliſhed actor and the ignorant ſpectator. Nothing can be pleaded in their behalf but preſcriptive right, the conſtant practice of the theatre. Shakſpeare lived in the infancy of the ſtage, when a rude audience demanded all the aſſiſtance which the poet could give them. He may be juſtified for calling up the ſpirit of Banquo, to raiſe feelings in the actor and terror in the ſpectator; but it is now time to try, at leaſt, what effect may be produced without ſuch ghoſtly aid.

Before Mr. Garrick diſplayed the terrible graces of action from the impreſſion of viſionary appearance, the comedians were ſtrangers to the effects which this ſcene could produce. Macbeth, they conſtantly exclaimed, was not a character of the firſt rate; all the pith of it was exhauſted, they ſaid, in the firſt and ſecond acts of the play. They formed their judgement from the drowſy and ineffectual manner of Garrick's predeceſſors, who could not force attention or applauſe from the audience during the three laſt acts. When Roſcius was informed what judgement the players had conceived of Macbeth, he ſmiled, and ſaid he ſhould be very unhappy if he were not able to keep alive the attention of the ſpectators to the laſt ſyllable of ſo animated a character.

This admirable ſcene was greatly ſupported by the ſpeaking terrors of Garrick's look and action. Mrs Pritchard ſhewed ad-

mirable

mirable art in endeavouring to hide Macbeth's frenzy from the obſervation of the gueſts, by drawing their attention to conviviality. She ſmiled on one, whiſpered to another, and diſtantly ſaluted a third; in ſhort, ſhe practiced every poſſible artifice to hide the tranſaction that paſſed between her huſband and the viſion his diſturbed imagination had raiſed. Her reproving and angry looks, which glanced towards Macbeth, at the ſame time were mixed with marks of inward vexation and uneaſineſs. When, at laſt, as if unable to ſupport her feelings any longer, ſhe roſe from her ſeat, and ſeized his arm, and, with a half-whiſper of terror, ſaid, '*Are you a man!*' ſhe aſſumed a look of ſuch anger, indignation, and contempt, as cannot be ſurpaſſed.

MACBETH.

It will have blood, they ſay: blood will have blood!

So in the Coœphoræ of Æſchylus:

There is a law, that, for each drop of blood
Shed on the earth, demands that blood be ſhed.

POTTER's ÆSCHYLUS.

IDEM.

——— My ſtrange and ſelf abuſe
Is the initiate fear that wants hard uſe:
We are but young in deed.

This is one, amongſt a thouſand other inſtances, of our author's great knowledge of nature. The criminal agent, when he has recovered from the terrors of his afflicted conſcience, ruſhes headlong into more guilt, by attributing his fears to any thing, except the real cauſe of them. Macbeth pacifies himſelf with this cordial, that his internal alarms are all owing to novelty of practice, and that perſiſting in evil would alone procure repoſe to his mind and ſtability to his government. So ſays Richard III.

Things bad begun make ſtrong themſelves by ill.

Scene V.

——— Get you gone,
And meet me in the pit of Acheron.

Shakſpeare, ſays Mr. Steevens, thought it allowable to beſtow the name of Acheron on any fountain, lake, or pit, through which

which there was ſuppoſed to be a communication between that river and the infernal regions; but Shakſpeare, I believe, did not know that, in the woods of Calder or Cawdor, there was a brook very near in name to that of the helliſh river. 'For, within thoſe woods, ſays Mr. Pennant, there are deep rocky glens, darkened with trees round each ſide of the wood; one has a great torrent roaring at its bottom, called the *brook of Acheneen:* it well merits the name of Acheron, being a moſt fit ſcene for witches to celebrate their nocturnal rites in.'*

Scene VI. Lenox and another lord.

This ſcene is left out in repreſentation, ſuppoſed to be unneceſſary to the plot of the play.

LENOX.

————————Did he not ſtrait,
In pious rage, the two delinquents tear
That were the ſlaves of drink and thralls of fear?

Lenox

* Pennant's Tour to Scotland. P. 124.

Lenox was preſent when Macbeth killed the ſleeping grooms, and, however better inſtructed he ſeems to be at preſent, he then juſtified the act, from the bloody daggers lying unwiped upon their pillows, and from their ſtaring and diſtracted looks; at the ſame time, ſaying,

No man's life was to be truſted with them.

IDEM.

——For, from broad hints and cauſe, he fail'd
His preſence at the tyrant's feaſt, I hear
Macduff lives in diſgrace.

The ſtory of Macduff and the tyrant's mutual jealouſy is related, after this manner, by Buchanan:

'For his better ſecurity, Macbeth was reſolved to build a caſtle on the high hill of Dunſinane, and to fortify it very ſtrongly. He ſummoned the thanes to aſſiſt in erecting the fortifications by turns. Macduff ſuſpected the king harboured ſome evil intentions towards him, and, though he ſent abundance of materials and labourers, with certain friends to quicken their operations,

operations, yet he would not attend in perſon. Macbeth, one day inſpecting the works, obſerved that a teem of oxen, ſent by Macduff, was unequal to the taſk of reaching the ſummit of the hill: upon this he took occaſion to ſay, that he was no ſtranger to the thane's contumacy and diſobedience, which he was determined to conquer, by fixing a yoke upon his own neck. Macduff, as ſoon as he was informed of this, immediately hired a veſſel, and ſet ſail to Lothian, and from thence he ſet out for England.'

CHAP-

CHAPTER XXVIII.

Incantation of witches. — Jonson's contention with Shakspeare. — Quotations from his Queen's Masque. — Speech of Macbeth to the presiding hags. — Invocation. — Hecate. — Attire of Johnson's witches. — King's evil. — Why confined to them. — Claim of the French kings from Clovis. — Queen-consorts never touched for the evil. — Lewis XI. *and St. Francis of Paul, their meeting.—Banishment of royal witchcraft. — Macduff's character. — Wilks, Booth, and Ryan.* — Hell is murky *explained. — English epicures. — Old enmity between the English and Scots. — Juvenal quoted. — Deportment of Macduff criticised. — Title of Thane, from Spelman, Buchanan, and Gurdon.*

Act IV. Scene I.

FIRST WITCH.

Thrice the brinded cat hath mew'd.

THE incantation, in this act, has been greatly celebrated, and, for boldneſs of invention, ſtrength of imagination, and propriety of conduct, is thought equal to any effort of our author's genius.

Mr. Malone has, with much probability, fixed the firſt repreſentation of Macbeth to the year 1606. However that may be, we are certain it was acted before Ben Jonſon produced his Maſque of Queens, which was exhibited before the king and queen in 1609. In that compoſition, there are many evident imitations of the magical inchantment in Macbeth. The ſucceſs of Shakſpeare alarmed the jealouſy of a man who fancied himſelf his rival, or rather his ſuperior. In this maſque, Jonſon has meaſured ſwords with our inimitable poet, and, to be juſt, we muſt own he has

has difplayed abundance of reading, and no mean vein of poetry. But, left I fhould fall under the charge of afferting what I cannot prove, I will prefent the reader with fome extracts from the Mafque, in which the imitator endeavours, though in vain, to conceal his obligations to the original.

Twelve hags bring their dame, who is fubftituted in the place of Hecate, an account of the ingredients which they have gathered to make the charm powerful. She fees them bufy, and cries out, almoft in the words of Shakfpeare, 'Well done, my hags!' She bids them relate what they have done.

FIRST HAG.

I have been all day looking after
A raven feeding upon a quarter.
As foon fhe turn'd her beak to the fouth,
I fnatch'd this morfel out of her mouth.

SECOND HAG.

I have been gathering wolves hairs,
The mad dog's foam, and the adder's ears.
The fpurging of a dead man's eyes,
And all fince the evening-ftar did rife.

SIXTH

SIXTH WITCH.

I had a dagger, what did I with that?
Kill'd an infant to have his fat.

TENTH.

I, from the jaws of a gardener's bitch,
Did ſnatch theſe bones, and then leapt a ditch,

ELEVENTH.

I went to the toad lives under the wall;
I charm'd him out, and he came to my call.
I ſcratch'd out the eyes of the owl before;
I tore the bat's wing: what have you more?

I ſhall cloſe my proofs with two quotations more. The abrupt, but ſublime, addreſs of Macbeth to the witches, in this fourth act, and an imitation of it ſpoken by the dame in the Maſque. The merit of both will plead in their behalf.

MACBETH.

How now, you ſecret, black, and midnight, hags!
I conjure you, by that which you profeſs,
Howe'er you come to know it, anſwer me;
Though you untie the winds, and let them fight
Againſt the churches: though the yeſty waves
Confound and ſwallow navigation up:

Though

Though bladed corn be lodg'd and trees blown down :
Though caſtles topple on their warders heads :
Though palaces and pyramids do ſlope
Their heads to their foundations : though the treaſure
Of nature's germins tumble all together,
E'en till deſtruction ſicken—Anſwer me
To what I aſk you !

The dame's invocation, from Jonſon.

You fiends and furies, if yet any be
Worſe than ourſelves, you that have quak'd to ſee
Theſe knots unty'd, and ſhrunk when we have
charm'd.
You, that, to arm us, have yourſelves diſarm'd,
And to our pow'rs reſign'd your whips and brands,
When we went forth the ſcourge of men and lands.
You that have ſeen me ride when Hecate
Durſt not take chariot ; when the boiſterous ſea,
Without a breath of wind, hath knock'd the ſky,
And that hath thunder'd, Jove not knowing why.
When we have ſet the elements at wars,
Made midnight ſee the ſun, and day the ſtars.
When the wing'd light'ning in the courſe hath ſtaid,
And ſwifteſt rivers have run back, afraid
To ſee the corn remove, the groves to range,
Whole places alter, and the ſeaſons change :
When the pale moon, at the firſt voice, down fell,
Poiſon'd, and durſt not ſtay the ſecond ſpell—
You that have oft been conſcious of theſe ſights,
And thou, thrice-formed ſtar, that, on theſe nights,

Art

Art only powerful, to whoſe triple name
Thus we incline, once, twice, and thrice, the ſame,
If now with rites profane and foul enough
We do invoke thee, darken all the roof,
With preſent fogs exhale earth's rott'neſt vapours,
And ſtrike a blindneſs through theſe blazing tapers, &c.

Notwithſtanding Jonſon, in the compoſition of this invocation, had the aſſiſtance of the antient poets whom he cites in his margin, it is little more than an amplification, or extended paraphraſe, of the ſpeech of Macbeth which I have juſt quoted. The word Hecate, which Shakſpeare abridges to two ſyllables, Jonſon, to ſhew his learning, reſtores to its ancient meaſure. The exordium of this piece, called the Maſque of Queens, celebrated from the houſe of fame, is very curious: 'His majeſty being ſet, and the whole company in full expectation, *the part of the ſcene which firſt preſented itſelf was an ugly hell, which, flaming beneath, ſmoked to the top of the roof.*' This was beating Shakſpeare's cauldron with a witneſs. The Witches were all differently attired; ſome with rats on their heads, ſome on their

 ſhoulders;

ſhoulders; others with ointment-pots at their girdles; all with ſpindles, timbrels, rattles, or other venefical inſtruments, making a confuſed noiſe, with ſtrange geſtures. The incantations of Shakſpeare, it is obſerved, are awfully tremendous; thoſe of other poets generally ridiculous.

Scene III.

MALCOLM.

Let us ſeek out ſome deſolate ſhade.

Mr. Steevens has quoted Hollingſhead's abridgement of a long diſcourſe between Malcolm and Macduff, from H. Boetius, on which this ſcene is founded. I think he might have ſhortened the margin very much, by tranſcribing Buchanan, who agrees with his countryman in the ſubject of the dialogue, but is more ſuccinct in the relation.

MALCOLM.

Why in that rawneſs left your wife and child?

The King, in Hamlet, act IV. condemns his own conduct, in privately burying

ing Polonius, in words of the ſame import:

We have done but greenly.

DOCTOR.

—— There are a crew of wretched ſouls
That ſtay his cure. ——
———— At his touch,
Such ſanctity hath heaven given his hand,
They preſently amend.

As the poet here intended a compliment to his royal maſter, it is moſt probable, that King James had, before the acting of this play, touched for the king's evil; nor can we ſuppoſe he would long defer aſſuming this power inherent in his predeceſſors.

The privilege of curing the king's evil is attributed only to kings. No other ſovereigns, of any degree, have laid claim to it. Why not give this power, ſays Voltaire, to emperors? and indeed, a fortiori, why is it not reſident in the popes? they are ſomething more than God's images upon earth; they are his vicars, his vicegerents. The ſame author ſuppoſes, that ſome viſionary, in order to make the baſtardy of William the Conqueror more reſpectable, beſtowed on him, as a gift from heaven, the power to cure the evil by a touch.

The kings of France could not, without a jealous eye, behold this extraordinary gift of celeſtial power in an Engliſh king, without putting in their claim to a ſimilar influence. It was therefore pretended, that they alſo, from their anceſtor, King Clovis, enjoyed the like gift of curing the king's evil.

Queen conſorts never pretended to this prerogative of the royal touch, becauſe their hands, it ſeems, were not anointed like thoſe of the kings; but Queen Elizabeth, being a ſovereign in her own right, cured thoſe, who were afflicted with this diſtemper, with great facility. It was happy for his ſubjects, that Lewis XI. of France, was not a freethinker; his avarice, tyranny, and oppreſſion, would then, perhaps, have been unlimited; but his groſs

groſs ſuperſtition was a check to his more dangerous vices, and the fear of damnation, in all probability, ſaved many an innocent life. Lewis, in order to remove the conſequences of an apoplexy, ſent for a famous man, called St. Francis of Paul, to cure him. Behold, when the ſaint arrived, he was terribly afflicted with the king's evil. Here Lewis had an opportunity to do one good turn for another; but it appeared, to all the world, that the king could neither cure the ſaint nor the ſaint the king. The courtiers, if they durſt, would have loudly laughed at them both.

The houſe of Brunſwick renounced all pretenſions to royal witchcraft; they claim no power of curing any diſtemper, by touch of hand, except avarice and ambition. Mr. Nichols, in his very entertaining notes to the anecdotes of Mr. Bowyer, has given, from undiſputed authority, the origin of this impoſture, which coſt ſome of our princes 3000l. per annum.

Queen Elizabeth was ſo peſtered with evil patients in her progreſs through Glouceſterſhire, that ſhe honeſtly told them, 'that God alone could relieve their complaints.' Our pious Charles II. touched no leſs than 92107 patients, between May 1661 and April 1682.*—Vide Anecdotes of Bowyer, p. 200.

MACDUFF.

He has no children! ——

If unſhaken loyalty, intrepidity of mind, and tenderneſs of heart, all united in an eminent degree, can diſtinguiſh a character, with ſubmiſſion to Dr. Johnſon, Macduff is by theſe qualities highly diſcriminated from others. He is, indeed, a proper contraſt to Macbeth, whoſe courage degenerates into frenzy.

We are told, by Colley Cibber, that Wilks had once an intention to reſign the part of Macduff, in which he had been much applauded, to an inferior actor, and that Booth had made an exchange of Banquo for this ſuperior character; but that the jealouſy

* At a guinea a touch, this would amount to a pretty large ſum; and hence we ſee the origin of this coſtly trick.

jealoufy of Booth's abilities had caufed Wilks to refume what he had fo indifcreetly given away. In the ftrong expreffion of horror on the murder of the King, and the loud exclamations of furprize and terror, Booth might have exceeded the utmoft efforts of Wilks. But, in the touches of domeftic woe, which require the feelings of the tender father and the affectionate hufband, Wilks had no equal. His fkill, in exhibiting the emotions of the overflowing heart with correfponding look and action, was univerfally admired and felt. His rifing, after the fuppreffion of his anguifh, into ardent and manly refentment, was highly expreffive of noble and generous anger.

We muft not forget Ryan's Macduff. --- In the reprefentation of this part, he had nothing to ftruggle with but the harfhnefs of his voice. He affumed fuch genuine terror and amazement, in the fecond act, as became the actor who was to impofe on the fpectator a belief of his having feen his royal mafter murdered! In the 4th act, he felt the loſs of his wife and children as became a father and a huſband. Ryan, we muſt own, was inferior to Wilks, but not in a degrading diſtance.

MALCOLM.

————Macbeth
Is ripe for ſhaking, and the powers above
Put on their inſtruments.

This paſſage is not, I think, well underſtood by Mr. Steevens, who interprets it, ‘ the heavenly powers encourage or thruſt forward their mortal inſtruments.’ But the author had a ſublimer meaning in this noble image: for it means,

Heaven itſelf is arming in our cauſe.

In the ſame ſenſe ſays Richard II.

For, every man, that Bolingbroke hath preſt
To lift ſhrewd ſteel againſt our golden crown,
Heaven, for his Richard, hath, in heavenly pay,
A glorious angel. Richard II. Act 3.

A ſimilar thought we find in the ſupplicants of Æſchylus, from the Chorus, ſpeaking of the inſcrutable power and wiſdom of Jove:

Though in majeſty enthron'd,
Thick clouds, and dark, incloſe him round,

As

As from the tower of heaven his eye
Surveys bold man's impiety;
Till, his ripe wrath on judgement bent,
He arms each god for puniſhment,
And from his high and awful throne,
Sends all his awful judgement down.

Potter's Æſchylus, Vol. I. p. 98.

Act V. Scene I.

Lady Macbeth walking in her ſleep.

LADY MACBETH.

Hell is murky!

Mr. Steevens ſuppoſes the Lady is talking to Macbeth, and here repeats this expreſſion as if it had come from him, in contempt of his cowardice! for, ſays he, ſhe would not have even hinted the terrors of hell to one whoſe conſcience ſhe ſaw was too much alarmed already for her purpoſe. This is certainly very ingenious; but, if we tread the ground over again, we ſhall find, that, in reaſoning about committing the murder of the King, the fear of hell had no weight with Macbeth. He ſays poſitively, that if, without the riſk of retaliation,

taliation, he could accomplifh the murder, he would hazard all fear of future retribution, *he would jump the life to come.* But, though the murderer fcorned to take the future world into his confideration, his Lady might think ferioufly of the pains of hell. Why elfe does fhe fay, ' Out, damned fpot!' why fo pathetically fpeak of ' the fmell of blood!' and tell us, that ' all the perfumes of Arabia will not fweeten her little hand!' and with 'a deep-fetched figh!' To reafon confequentially upon what efcapes from a perfon, difturbed in imagination and diftracted with guilt, is not an eafy tafk: but, if we muft apply, in this cafe, to fober argument, ' Hell is murky' would be a natural and fearful fuggeftion to one who had committed the worft of crimes, and had not quarrelled with her creed. The fcene is compofed of disjointed thoughts and unconnected ideas, like the picture of a ftorm, by a great mafter, where the wreck is varioufly fcattered to fhew its terrible effects.

Scene

Scene II.

LENOX.

> ——— There is Siward's ſon,
> And many unrough youths that even now
> Proteſt their firſt of manhood.

Something very ſimilar to this we read in Richard II. act the 3d, in Scrope's ſpeech to the King:

> ——— Boys, with womens voices,
> Strive to ſpeak big, and claſp their female joints
> In ſtiff unweildy arms againſt thy crown.

Scene III.

MACBETH.

> ——— Then fly, falſe thanes,
> And mingle with the Engliſh epicures.

It is an old obſervation, that England is one great cook's ſhop; and our neighbours muſt confeſs, that in no other country are the means of gratifying the appetite to be obtained ſo plentifully. To a traveller, in England, no ſights preſent themſelves ſo frequently to his view as a variety of large convenient

convenient inns, and houſes that furniſh good entertainment. Not to contradict any of the commentators, whoſe remarks on this paſſage are very reaſonable, I ſhall only obſerve, that Macbeth lays hold of the vulgar prejudices of his countrymen, againſt their ſouthern neighbours, to ſerve his preſent purpoſe. The reproach of *epicures*, in plainer terms, *Engliſh poke-pudding tikes*, or *Engliſh bag-pudding dogs*, is as old, I believe, as the enmity between the two nations, and one which the lower claſs, or vulgar Scots, uſed to throw on the Engliſh. The frequent ſkirmiſhes, between the borderers of both kingdoms, ſerved to keep alive that hateful animoſity which the Union itſelf could ſcarcely extinguiſh. The diverſions of children were expreſſive of national ſtrife. The young Scots had formerly a game called Engliſhmen and Scotchmen: one ſide was called Scotch, and the other Engliſh. They took off their upper garments, and laid them ſeverally in heaps; that ſide, which plundered the other of moſt clothes,

won

won the game. This indeed was particularly expreſſive of the war, for booty, carried on near the borders.

The Engliſh were a match for their neighbours in illiberal taunts and ſcurrilous reproaches, from which even our parliament was not entirely free; for, when James I. propoſed to unite the two kingdoms, ſeveral members of the lower houſe treated his offer in terms of the moſt ſignificant contempt. In a ſarcaſtic ſpeech, which Oſborne has preſerved, the Scots were termed, ' ſons of the locuſts and daughters of the horſe-leech.'

The Ombi and Tentyritæ, two nations of Egypt, were not more averſe from one another, on account of the former loving crocodiles, and the other hating them, than the Engliſh and Scots were, perhaps for a reaſon equally ridiculous.

Inter finitimos vetus atque antiqua ſimultas,
Immortale odium et nunquam ſanabile vulnus,
Ardet adhuc, Ombos et Tentyra: ſummus utrinque
Inde furor vulgo, quod numina vicinorum

Odit

Odit uterque locus, cum ſolos credat habendos
Eſſe deos quos ipſe colit.

Juvenal, Sat. 15.

MACBETH.

——— She ſhould have died hereafter;
There would have been a time for ſuch a word!

Macbeth's confidence of victory, in the enſuing conteſt with Malcolm, was raiſed to the higheſt pitch, by the prophecies of Birnam wood and his not being to be ſlain by one that was born of woman. In conſequence of this opinion, he ſeems to wiſh that his Lady had died at a more quiet and leſs buſy time than the preſent. —— 'There would have been a time for ſuch a word,' is ſpoken in the ſame ſenſe with that which Brutus ſpeaks over the dead body of Caſſius: 'Caſſius, I ſhall find time, I ſhall find time.' 'Had ſhe died after my victory, I could then have paid that reſpect to her memory which I ought.' This explanation is, in general, I believe, conformable to that of Dr. Johnſon on the ſame paſſage.

IDEM.

IDEM.

And that which ſhould accompany old age,
As honour, love, obedience, troops of friends,
I muſt not look to have!

Dr. Johnſon thinks the courage of Macbeth preſerves ſome eſteem; but that quality he had in common with Banquo and others. I am of opinion, that his extreme reluctance to murder his royal maſter, his uncommon affliction of mind after he had perpetrated the crime, with the perpetual revolt of his conſcience upon the commiſſion of each new act of cruelty, are the qualities which render Macbeth, though not worthy of our eſteem, yet an object not entirely unmeriting our pity, in ſpite of his ambition and cruelty.

MACBETH.

——— Fear not, till Birnam-wood
Do come to Dunſinane.

Birnam-wood, ſays Mr. Pennant, ſeems not to have recovered the march of its anceſtors to Dunſinane; but there are ſtill to be be ſeen ſome remains of Macbeth's caſtle on this high hill.

Scene VI.

MACDUFF.

Make all our trumpets ſpeak, give them all breath.

This and the following line ſeem to be allotted to Macduff purely to ſupport his conſequence; for, according to the rules of propriety, the commanding officer, Malcolm, ſhould have given this charge.

The moſt difficult part, an actor has to ſuſtain, conſiſts in proper action, look, and deportment, when he does not ſpeak. I ſcarcely remember to have ſeen any exhibitor of Macduff who had not entirely forgotten, by the tranquillity and tameneſs of his behaviour, the ſtorm which had ſhaken his whole frame in the preceding act. This is his firſt appearance after the ſad information of his murdered wife and children: ſhould he not, by his look, convince the ſpectators that he had not loſt the remembrance

remembrance of all that was dear to him? ſhould not his countenance be impreſſed with grief and reſentment; nay, with impatience, too, to take revenge on the man who had ſo ſenſibly injured him? Wilks was the only Macduff I can recollect who ſeemed to have a tolerable notion of his ſituation; nor indeed did *he*, in deportment, anſwer the idea of what he ſhould feel on the occaſion.

MALCOLM.

——— My *thanes* and kinſmen,
Henceforth be earls.

The title of *thane* was not confined to Scotland, but common to the ſouthern, as well as northern, part of the iſland. —— '*Thanorum* appellatio in uſu fuit poſt adventum Normanorum, ut a Domeſday liqueat,' ſays Spelman in his Gloſſary. —— Leſly, de Origine Moribus, &c. Scotorum, has the following paſſage, quoted by the ſame author: 'Nam in ipſis reipublicæ noſtræ rudimentis, cum aliqua adhuc barbaries Scotiam occupaſſet, quoſdam duces,

 thanos,

thanos, vernacula lingua vocabant; illuſtri familia ortos delegerunt, quibus ſe ſuamque familiam regendam committebant.' --- And Buchanan: ' Superioribus ſæculis, præter *thanos*, hoc eſt, præfectos regionum, ſive monarchas, &c. nullum honoris nomen equeſtri ordine altius.'

Gurdon, in his Hiſtory of court-baron and court-leet, gives a very copious account of the origin and dignity of the Engliſh *thane*. I ſhall quote his definition of the word, and ſomething relating to the *thane*'s power and juriſdiction; but muſt refer the reader to the book itſelf for farther information:

' The Saxon word *thane*, or *thegne*, implies *miniſter*, or *ſervant*; one who was an honorary ſervant to the king in the field and in council, not a ſervant under abſolute command, but obliged, by fœderal union, to ſerve the king in war and council, of one and the other's property.' Gurdon's parliaments, &c. p. 537.

' The

'The *thane* had the ſame juriſdiction in his ſoke, or manor, as the king had in his great ſigniory; but neither of them were abſolute. The king, in the great ſigniory, determined by and with the advice of his *thanes*, as original ſharers with the king in the conquered lands; and the *thane*, in the court of his ſoke, or little ſigniory, determined all differences between his men in their civil rights, and alſo puniſhed criminals, with the advice and conſent of his freemen. Life and death were at firſt within the juriſdiction of the *thane*'s hall-mote.' Ibidem.

To paſs by unnoticed the obſervations of the accompliſhed Mrs. Montague, on Macbeth, would be uncandid and unjuſt. Her reflections are the product of mature and ſolid judgement, conveyed in language at once forcible and elegant.

Julius Cæſar.

CHAPTER XXIX.

Shakſpeare's predilection for Brutus. — His character of Cæſar. —Cæſar's weakneſs. — The reception of Julius Cæſar *when originally acted. — Leonard Diggs. — Hart and Mohun, their excellence in Brutus and Caſſius. — Rymer's opinion of their ſkill. — Lord Rocheſter's character of Mohun. — Duke of Buckingham's Cæſar and Brutus. — Voltaire's Mort de Céſar.—Abbé de Fontaines. — Hill's Roman Revenge. — Quotation from it. — Shakſpeare unjuſtly criticiſed. — Roman and Engliſh mechanics alike. — A muleteer made a tribune of Rome. — Honour in one hand and death in the other. — Caſſius's character. — Winſtone, Quin, Mills, Milward, and W. Mills. —* Julius Cæſar *not acted under Garrick's management.*

ment. — Why. — Q. Ligarius. — Bowman. — Quin jealous of his applauſe. — Roman actors. — Their indefatigable application. — Nero, an actor. — His fear of an audience. — Æſopus and Roſcius. — The public ſpirit of Æſopus. — Players muſt obey audiences. — The Roman ear delicate. — Æſopus obliged to obſerve the powers of his voice. — Roman actors limited to particular parts. — Æſopus. — Moliere and Colley Cibber. — Riches of a Roman actor. — Roſcius, a rival of Cicero in geſticulation. — A great teacher of acting. — Roman ſlaves. — Cicero's character of Roſcius.

THE tragedy of Julius Cæſar ſeems to have been written by Shakſpeare with a deſign to introduce his favourite character of Brutus. The author, who had carried the notions of indefeaſible right, of paſſive obedience, and non-reſiſtance, in many parts of his works, as far as any of the politicians and divines of his time; in this play ſeems to have adopted more liberal principles of government, and to have indulged ſentiments purely democratical. As he drew his knowledge of Roman characters from Plutarch, it is ſurpriſing he ſhould have drawn ſo deficient a portrait of Cæſar. Little of it has he preſerved except his undaunted courage and attractive urbanity. He has likewiſe not forgotten his contempt of dreams, omens, forebodings, and every ſpecies of ſuperſtition. But the poet has made him, what he never was, an oſtentatious boaſter, and a violent rejector of the petitions addreſſed to him. But perhaps Cæſar was to be leſſened in order to aggrandize Brutus.

It muſt however be ſaid, in excuſe of our great dramatiſt, that he has confined himſelf to that period of time, immediately preceding the death of the dictator. For his original, Plutarch, relates that his conduct then was of a different complexion from what it had formerly been. Succeſs ſeems to have rendered Cæſar forgetful of his ſituation; and his behaviour to the ſenate, in

not

not rising up to salute them when they approached him, was justly reprehensible. But his passion for the kingly title, so odious to his countrymen, was a glaring proof of his imbecility; since he possessed all the power of royalty under a title less obnoxious to censure, that of Dictator. The preserving the names of old titles, and offices, is the least compliment, that he, who seizes the supreme power, can pay to the manes of departed liberty; and this artful behaviour has often established more firmly a new system of government raised upon the ruins of the old. Though Shakspeare has put into the mouth of Cæsar more than usual severity of expression in rejecting the petition and intreaties of Metellus Cimber in behalf of his brother, yet there is sufficient ground in Plutarch to suppose, that the persisting clamours of the conspirators drew from him an answer of more than usual asperity. But indeed Plutarch himself is accused, by his last translators, of giving a very imperfect draft of Cæſar's character.

Notwithſtanding Nat. Lee, in his dedication of his Junius Brutus, has aſſerted that the Brutus of our author could, with much ado, beat himſelf into the heads of a blockiſh age: we have authority, from two copies of verſes written by Leonard Diggs, prefixed to the plays and the ſonnets of Shakſpeare, that the audience were in raptures with the play of Julius Cæſar, and more eſpecially with the admired ſcene, in Act IV. between Brutus and Caſſius:

> —— Till I hear a ſcene more nobly take
> Than when *the half-ſword playing Romans ſpake.*
>
> Works of Shakſpeare, 1623.

> So I have ſeen, when Cæſar would appear,
> And on the ſtage at half-ſword parley were
> Brutus and Caſſius! *O! how the audience*
> *Were raviſh'd! with what wonder went they hence!*
>
> Shakſpeare's ſonnets, 1640.

Dryden himſelf confeſſes he was fired with this noble ſcene, and aſhamed of his own

own want of genius to rival Shakſpeare. But Brutus could be no favourite in the reign of Charles II. when government was a factious conſpiracy againſt the rights of the people, and every friend of liberty was branded as a fomenter of ſedition. However, Julius Cæſar, amongſt the few plays of our great poet which were revived ſoon after the Reſtoration, was one ſelected from the royal liſt given the players of the King's Theatre in Drury Lane, by Hart and Mohun, in which they greatly ſignalized themſelves, and eſpecially Mohun, who, for his excellent performance of Caſſius, is commended by Downs, the ſtage-hiſtorian, and ſtill, to his greater honour, applauded by Lord Rocheſter. That we have no memoirs or relations but what can be gathered from Downs, and ſome traditional ſcraps and ſlight notices of poets and critics of theſe two great actors, is to be lamented. Their rank in life, having both been honoured with commands in the army, placed them above their fellows. Rymer, the

the celebrated critic and hiſtoriographer, has applauded them highly for their wonderful power of fixing the attention of the audience, and ſpeaking to them as much by action as utterance. Mohun was particularly remarkable for the dignity of his deportment and graceful manner of treading the ſtage. The Earl of Rocheſter reproaches the comedians of the Duke of York's company for their vain attempts to ape his excellences, and ridiculing his defects, the conſequences of age and infirmity.

Yet theſe are they who durſt expoſe the age
Of the great wonder of the Engliſh ſtage,
Whom nature ſeem'd to form for your delight,
And bade him ſpeak, as ſhe bade Shakſpeare write:
Theſe blades indeed are cripples in their art,
Mimic the foot, but not the ſpeaking part;
Let them the Traitor or Volpone try:
——————— Could they ——
Rage like Cethegus, or like Caſſius die?

Sheffield Duke of Buckingham, obſerving there was a double plot in this play, ſat down to form two tragedies out of one, Julius

Julius Cæſar, and the death of Marcus Brutus. Whether they are ſtrictly conformable to the rules of the drama, and obſerve the unities, I have not ſo critically examined them as to determine, but he ſeems to have taken great pains to extinguiſh the noble fire of the original. The ſtyle, except where Shakſpeare is preſerved, is correctly cold, and regularly dull, uninformed by the ſpirit of genius to give life to the whole maſs. His grace has introduced upon the ſtage what our poet has only related, Cæſar's refuſal of the crown offered to him by Mark Antony at the Lupercal games. The account of this tranſaction, by Caſca in the original, is humourouſly circumſtantial, but the exhibition of it on the ſtage, in the new Julius Cæſar, is tedious and proſaic. The reader may judge from a ſhort ſpecimen of it.

Antony preſenting Julius Cæſar with the crown.

Hail! mighty man, thou godlike Cæſar hail!
Stoop to our wiſhes, and vouchſafe to wear

This

This crown, prefented thee by all mankind:
Shine on us like the fun in his full luftre,
Adorn us with your power, and make us proud
Of being fubjects to fo great a king.

C Æ S A R.

I am not call'd your king, but your dictator,
A name I hope that bears as great a found,
Therefore, I both refufe and flight the crown,
Which can add nothing to my power or Rome's:
[*Cæfar puts back the crown, and the people fhout.*]
I am glad, my friends, you are fo eafily pleas'd
With my refufing what I think below me, &c.

The whole fcene is written in the fame frigid manner; the reader will find that Buckingham is feldom warmed with the bright blaze of the original, which, like the veftal virgin, he had taken in his cuftody to preferve and cherifh.

La Mort de Céfar of Voltaire is one of the leaft valuable of all this great writer's dramatic pieces. From a hatred, I fuppofe, of republican freedom, he has adopted the ftory of Brutus being Cæfar's fon by Servilia, the fifter of Cato. But the improbability

probability of this ſtory is evident from Cæſar's being little more than fourteen years of age when Brutus was born. Voltaire's tragedy is in three acts; without women, and conſequently free from love: how he could ſuppoſe a play, deficient in ſuch eſſentials, could pleaſe ſo gay a nation as the French, is not very eaſy to imagine. I do not remember that the Greeks, whom the French profeſs to follow, have any tragedy without females, except the Philoctetes of Sophocles. The Abbé de Fontaines, a mercenary writer, in a periodical work of which he had the direction, attacked with acrimony La Mort de Céſar: Voltaire was alarmed, but found an infallible method of ſoftening this Cerberus; for the abbé ſometime after pretended that he had been unhappily miſled, by the errors of the preſs, to cenſure a play of ſuch uncommon merit; for ſuch, ſays he, I found it, after peruſing a true copy of the original.

Aaron Hill formed his Roman Revenge upon Voltaire's Death of Cæſar.— But he much

much enlarged and improved the plan, not only by the addition of two characters, Calphurnia and Portia, but with a number of others, besides great variety of action. Hill seems to have idolized the character of Cæsar, whom he drew in the most amiable colours, representing him to be the worthiest and most amiable of men. The same fondness for monarchical principles, which misled Voltaire to make Brutus the son of Cæsar, infected Hill, who has adopted the same idle tale; the father breaks the secret to the son, who receives it with surprise and dread, but, after much struggling between nature and principle, and a long suspence between the love of liberty and the horror of destroying a parent, he is yet impelled, by the artful contrivance of the conspirators and his own enthusiastic notions of Rome and liberty, to become an associate in Cæsar's murder. This play, though strongly recommended and approved by Lord Bolingbroke and Mr Pope, did not please the managers

managers or actors. Neither Quin nor Garrick could be prevailed upon to act this demi-god, Cæsar. And indeed, although there are many admirable sentiments and some affecting scenes in the Roman Revenge, it is so stiffened with epithet, bespangled with antithesis, and decorated with pointed thought, all which he has marked in Italic letters, that the players would have found it very difficult to utter the lines trippingly, as Shakspeare says, from the tongue; the audience would not have relished a Brutus so differently drawn from that of their favourite Shakspeare; neither would they have borne with a patriot who could lift the murdering sword against his own father. The reader will judge of the style from a short specimen taken from a scene, where the father and son plead in behalf of their different forms of government.

CÆSAR.

Rome's senate, rich and proud, oppress'd her people:
Her people, poor and head-strong, spurn'd their yoke:
Hence

Hence rose the new necessity, thou know'st not,
Of some unformal self-supporting *sword*,
To cut sedition boldly *to the root*,
And rectify the crooked growth of empire:
This done, *degen'rate* Rome grows fit for liberty;
Make it thy future gift and therefore reign.
Now 'tis sedition's cloak, her trumpet's *call*.

BRUTUS.

——— Teach the senate
These fond defects, and shape their wish'd redress:
Their's is the right to think for *council'd Rome*.
Cæsar a king! were all his virtues stars,
Rome's rights invading makes his virtues crimes.
Cæsar's a citizen, protecting law,
Mix'd with the people, reigns the people's god.

Act I. Scene I.

Flavius, Marcellus, and other Commoners.

Shakspeare is accused of giving the manners of London to the inhabitants of any other part of the globe to which he transports his spectators: what! says the critic, compare the Roman citizens to an English mob, by giving them the rude behaviour of our artisans? Had not then the Romans

mans carpenters, bricklayers, and ſhoemakers, as well as ourſelves? The Roman populace were not a whit more poliſhed than our own. It is natural for every mechanic to talk in the language of his own trade, like the honeſt cobler in this ſcene, who ingenuouſly tells the tribunes, he leads the people up and down the ſtreets of Rome to wear out their ſhoes, that he may have more work. I have ſeen old Ben Jonſon, the player, perſonate this little part with great humour.

Theſe gentlemen, who think the great maſters of the world were too polite and well-bred to be repreſented like our Engliſh mechanics, ſhould read ſome of Cicero's epiſtles, and more eſpecially his oration in defence of Publius Sextius againſt Clodius: there they will find more wickedneſs, outrage, and miſchief, perpetrated by Clodius's mob, than he ever heard was committed by an Engliſh rabble. He will be convinced, too, that the Romans were as vulgar and boiſterous, and much more corrupt, and ſelfiſh, than our own people.

A muleteer was, by an odd viciſſitude of fortune, advanced to the dignity of a Roman tribune; this fellow was employed by Clodius, as a fit agent, to promote his riot; but his own people having, as they imagined, killed a tribune of the oppoſite party, Clodius determined to make the matter even by ſacrificing the life of the muleteer; but he, apprehending the danger, had recourſe to his old habit of mule-driving, and, with a baſket on his head, eſcaped the intended aſſaſſination.

BRUTUS.

Set honour in one eye and death in the other,
And I will look on *both indifferently* ———
For let the Gods ſo ſpeed me as I love
The name of honour more than I fear death.

Dr. Warburton, inſtead of *both indifferently*, reads *death indifferently*. Dr. Johnſon ſupports with great plauſibility the other reading. *Indifferently*, I think, in this place, means, I will conſider both with *coolneſs* and *impartiality*. Buck-

ingham

ingham has, in my opinion, rather mangled than improved the ſenſe of the author in this place:

Set virtue in one eye, and let grim death
Shake his unheeded dart, I'll ſtill be fix'd;
For may the Gods ſo help me, as for honour
I look indifferently on life and death.

Quin, I remember, ſpoke the word in diſpute as Warburton altered it.

CASCA.

You pull'd me by the cloak, would you ſpeak with me?

During the ſcene in which Caſca relates the behaviour of Cæſar in the lupercal games, where Antony offers him the crown, the character of the relater is ſupported with great humour. In act II. he unexpectedly appears a different man: however the author has juſtified this conduct from the mouth of Caſſius, who tells us, that his dogged manner was not his own, but aſſumed. The poet, having no buſineſs for Caſca after the murder of Cæſar, has dropt him in act III. but the players, finding their company not numerous enough to ſupply all the characters of this play, many years ſince enlarged Caſca, by adding to his part what belongs to Titinius. Julius Cæſar was one of the three plays acted by the deſire of the prime nobility in Queen Anne's time, with the united ſtrength of the then two companies. Caſca, if I remember right, was acted by a principal comedian. Above five and forty years ſince, Winſtone was ſelected for that character, when Quin acted Brutus, and the elder Mills Caſſius, Milward M. Antony, and W. Mills Julius Cæſar. The aſſumed doggedneſs and ſourneſs of Caſca ſat well upon Winſtone. The four principal parts have not ſince that time been equally preſented. Mr Garrick, pleaſed with the ſpirit and fire of Caſſius, once determined to have tried his ſkill in that part; but, whether he thought he ſhould only ſwell the conſequence of his competitor Quin in Brutus, or from what other cauſe, I know not, he relinquiſhed his intention:

nor

nor was this excellent play revived during his management of the ſtage, though I am of opinion he wanted not actors of merit to do conſiderable juſtice to the play.

Scene VI.

Caſca and Cicero.

So important a man as Cicero ſhould not have been introduced in a ſcene of ſo little ſignification as the relation of a prodigy. The players have very judiciouſly left it out in the repreſentation.

Act II. Scene I.

BRUTUS.

——O! Conſpiracy —— by day
Where wilt thou find a cavern deep enough
To maſk thy monſtrous viſage? Seek none, Conſpiracy!
Hide it in ſmiles and affability.——

Sentiments like theſe are not unfrequent in Shakſpeare: Brutus repeats the ſame once or twice in this very ſcene. So, when Macbeth has determined to murder his royal maſter, he reſolves to hide his dark intention by diſſembled courteſy and over-acted ſhow of duty.

—— Away, and mock the time with faireſt ſhow;
Falſe face muſt hide what the falſe heart doth know.

Macbeth, Act 2d.

CAIUS LIGARIUS [to BRUTUS.]

———— Set on your foot,
And, with a heart new fir'd, I'll follow you
To do I know not what, but it ſufficeth
That Brutus leads me on.

Bowman, who had acted this part of Ligarius more than fifty years, was advanced above the age of fourſcore when I ſaw him perform it; he aſſumed great vigour and a truly Roman ſpirit. The applauſe which he obtained, and juſtly merited, was not reliſhed by Quin, who neglected to pay that attention to the character which he ought. This is a fault which I have obſerved in ſome principal actors, who have treated their inferiors of the ſtage with diſregard, becauſe they were below them in rank as comedians, though the parts they acted demanded

manded obſervance to be paid them, at leaſt before the public, to ſupport that ſtage-deception, without which a play loſes its effect.

BRUTUS.

Let not our looks put on our purpoſes;
But bear it, as our Roman actors do,
With untir'd ſpirits and formal conſtancy.

Whether Shakſpeare intended in theſe lines to celebrate the perſevering labour and indefatigable ſpirit of the actor in general, or the Roman actor in particular, is perhaps doubtful. That the ſkill of the latter was put to a much ſeverer trial than that of a modern comedian cannot well be denied. It is much eaſier to pleaſe, I ſhould imagine, ſixteen or ſeventeen hundred perſons, ſhut up in a ſmall building, than ſixty or ſeventy thouſand ſpectators who behold a play from a ſpacious amphitheatre. But to drop this argument, which is perhaps more ſpecious than ſolid, we have good authority to ſay that the Roman actors were uncommonly ſolicitous to pleaſe their judges, and extremely fearful of incurring their diſpleaſure. Nero, when he acted a part on the ſtage, felt the greateſt anxiety leſt he ſhould be ſubject to the diſpleaſure of the ſpectators.

Suetonius, in the life of this emperor, relates, that, during the time of the repreſentation, he obſerved the laws of the theatre ſo punctually, that he never ventured to ſpit, nor to wipe off the ſweat from his forehead except with his elbow. As he was once acting in a tragedy he let his ſtaff, or truncheon, fall out of his hand; and, though he recovered it immediately, his terror and affright were ſo great, leſt he ſhould be hiſſed off the ſtage, that he could not compoſe himſelf, till one of the players ſwore no notice was taken of it, amidſt the noiſe and acclamations of the people.

The very dreſs of the Roman actor was, from the richneſs of habit and variety of ornament, in the characters of heroes and demi-gods, a perfect burthen to the wearer. To appear like Hercules, he muſt be ſtuffed

ſtuffed in the body and raiſed upon elevated buſkins. The *niti cothurno* of Horace has its literal, as well as metaphorical, meaning; to walk gracefully upon ſuch ſupporters muſt have required great practice and much art. The maſque, too, covered the head and ſhoulders, and was adorned with large plumage and other decorations.

Cicero has given honourable teſtimony of the two celebrated Roman actors, Æſopus and Roſcius, men whom he ranked in the number of his friends, and ſtyled his *Deliciæ*. To the former, indeed, he was indebted for the foundation of his eloquence; by his leſſons he attained to that conſummate art in ſpeaking, which rendered him the firſt orator of his time.* But Æſopus was not more admired for his ſkill in his profeſſion than for the love he bore his country, and for inviolable attachment to his friend. During

* Melworth's Epiſtles of Cicero, vol. I. p. 119. The Grecian actors were ſtill more accompliſhed than the Romans. Hiſtriones Græci plerumque erant homines docti, et ingenui oratores et poetæ, et in artibus aliis ſpectabiles. G. I. Voſſius, Inſt. Poetic.

During Cicero's exile, and at a time when his friends had procured a decree of the ſenate for his recal from baniſhment, Æſopus, ſays Cicero, who performed the ſame good part in public which he did upon the ſtage, was acting the part of Telamon, who was baniſhed from his country, in one of Accius's plays. By the particular emphaſis of his voice, and a change of a word or two in ſome of the lines, he dextrouſly contrived to turn the thoughts of the audience upon Cicero. —— *What he! who always ſtood up for the republic! — Who in doubtful times ſpared neither life nor fortune! —The firmeſt friend in the moſt imminent danger! — Of ſuch parts and talents! — O father! — I ſaw his houſe and rich furniture all in flames!* — By peculiar addreſs the actor ſo managed, that at the end of every ſentence the applauſes were inceſſant: and, in another tragedy of the ſame author, called Brutus,† when, inſtead of *Brutus*, Æſopus

† Cicero pro P. Sextio. — Middleton's life of Cicero, vol. I.

Æſopus pronounced *Tullius*, who eſtabliſhed the liberty of his citizens, the people were ſo affected, they called for it again a thouſand times.

And here I cannot help obſerving, that the player, as the ſervant and creature of the public, ought not to refuſe repeating any line or ſentence that he has once pronounced on the ſtage, when demanded by the ſpectators. Much has been ſaid, in a late ſtage-hiſtory,‡ of the folly of an audience, in exacting the reiteration of ſome particular lines in the tragedy of Mahomet acted on the Dublin theatre ſome years ſince, and which were applied to the politics of the times. If there be really any abſurdity in the caſe, it lies at the door of thoſe who can beſt anſwer it, the people aſſembled in the theatre. To hazard the diſpleaſure of thoſe, who have the power to inforce their orders, is equally impolitic and dangerous; as the manager of the Dublin theatre found it, to his great damage.

Notwithſtanding

‡ Victor's Hiſtory of the Stage.

Notwithſtanding the high eſtimation in which Æſopus was held with the public, ſo nice and delicate was the Roman ear, that he durſt not venture to exhibit with the ſmalleſt defect in his power of utterance or the leaſt approach to hoarſeneſs. If the modulation of his voice was diſturbed by a cold, or any accidental impediment, they immediately reproved him by evident marks of their diſpleaſure. The nurſing of the voice was attended with particular ſolicitude by the Roman actors,* and certain regulations were formed to manage its various inflections. Beſides this, the poet gave the actor certain rules in writing, like notes in muſic, by which the tones of his voice, in uttering either ſentiment or paſſion, were to be governed. The actors were circumſcribed too within the limits of their particular talents and abilities: thoſe, whoſe voices could reach the extent of paſſion, acted parts of

* Cicero de Oratore.

of loud vehemence; thoſe, who excelled chiefly in action and deportment, were directed to ſuitable characters. Æſopus, ſays Cicero, did not often try the difficult part of Ajax.*

This great actor, ſeveral years after he had quitted the ſtage, in a very advanced time of life, was called upon to honour the opening of Pompey's theatre with his performance; but unhappily he only expoſed his imbecility, and was diſmiſſed with pity. Æſopus, attempting to pronounce a ſolemn oath, his voice failed him, and he could not utter diſtinctly the words, *Si ſciens fallo.* Moliere, in ſpite of a decaying conſtitution and a nervous habitual cough, would, in contradiction to the remonſtrances of his friends, perſiſt to act, as this amiable man declared, for the good of his people. In his laſt play of the Hypochondriac he was ſeized with a convulſion, in pronouncing the word *juro*, and died a few days after.—About

† Cicero de Officiis.

About the time Mr. Garrick charmed the public with Shakſpeare's character of Richard III. Colley Cibber in his old age was impelled by his vanity to reſume the part, to which, notwithſtanding all that he and his friends have ſaid about his performance of it, he was by no means equal; for his cracked pipe could not give force to the animated ſcenes of the two laſt acts of Richard III. Cibber's ſucceſs was little better than that of Æſopus; he was diſmiſſed indeed, like the Roman actor, with no marks of diſpleaſure; but mere ſufferance, in ſuch a ſituation, is rather an humiliating circumſtance. Victor, who ſaw him when the play was over, told me that Colley confeſſed he never longed ſo much for any thing as the dying ſcene of Richard. Macklin indeed acted the ſame part at ſeventy-five with as ſtrong a voice as he was maſter of at forty-five; but where ſhall we find two Macklins?

Æſopus died immenſely rich; Melmoth eſtimates his property at 200000l. I ſhould imagine it to be twice as much; for if he could

could give a feaſt, as we are informed he did, at which one diſh alone coſt him near 4900l. what muſt be the amount of the whole?

But the abilities of Roſcius ſeem to have exceeded thoſe of his friend Æſopus. So well did he underſtand the various powers of action, that he conteſted with Cicero to expreſs as perfectly by geſture as the orator could by elocution. His character is ſo well known, that I ſhall dwell the leſs upon it.

Notwithſtanding his perverſe or ſquinting eyes, the Romans were better pleaſed with him when he played without a maſk than with one.† He was a great teacher of the art of acting, and acquired great riches by it. For, of all the Roman ſlaves, thoſe, who were capable of being taught to act, brought their maſters the largeſt profit.* Slaves who could read were ſold, according to Dr. Arbuthnot, at 807*l.* 5*s.* 10*d.*

† Cicero. * Plinii Nat. Hiſt. lib. x.

10*d*. We may guefs from thence the value of the others. Rofcius was fo hard to pleafe, that he declared, he never could find a pupil whom he entirely approved; not but that he had the inftruction of many youths of very great abilities; but his confummate knowledge could difcover defects unperceived by every body elfe. When he was advanced to old age, he changed his mode of recitation; he fpoke not with the fame rapidity as formerly; his tones were then more foft and deliberate, and the mufic was accommodated to the voice. In his Oration for Archias, the poet, Cicero embraces an opportunity to pay refpect to the memory of Rofcius. 'Where amongft us,' fays the Orator, 'is the mind fo barbarous, where is the heart fo unfeeling, as to be unaffected with the death of Rofcius?' He died indeed in a very advanced age, but he was a man who by his art and elegance feemed to challenge immortality to his perfon. Q. Catulus

Catulus pronounced this man to be more beautiful than the riſing ſun, notwithſtanding his ſquinting eyes and his diſtorted looks.

Conſtiteram, exorientem Auroram forte ſalutans,
Cum ſubito a læva Roſcius exoritur.
Pace mihi liceat, cœleſtes, dicere veſtra,
Mortalis viſu'ſt pulchrior eſſe Deo.

Huic, Deo pulchrior. —— At erat, ſicut hodie eſt, perverſiſſimis oculis.

Q. Catulus apud Ciceronem de Nat. Deorum.

CHAPTER XXX.

Cæſar's urbanity. — Queſtion of Cæſar's death. — The oppreſſive ſpirit of the ſenate.—Ariſtocracy and oligarchy. — Tiberius and Caius Gracchus. — Number of Roman citizens when Cæſar was murdered. — Panem et circenſes. — Cæſar's abilities. — His clemency. — Perfidy of conſpirators. — Romans diſqualified to entertain freedom. — Number of ſlaves in Rome. — Rich furniture and buildings of the Romans. — Luxury of the Romans. — Price of a mullus. — Son of Æſopus. — His profuſeneſs. — The pleaſure of ſeeing fiſh expire. — Difficulty in repreſenting the aſſaſſination of Cæſar.— Actors of Julius Cæſar. — Goodman, Colley Cibber, and the Dutcheſs of Cleveland. — Alexander the Great. — Goodman a highwayman. — Antony's ſervant, and Brutus. — Wilks's action. — Speech of Antony.

— *Antony*

— *Antony well paid for his oratory.* — *Isocrates and Demosthenes.* — *Defects of Wilks.* — *Barry's powers.* — *Milward's excellences.* — *The word* villain. — Baite *and* bay. — *Brutus and Cassius.* — *Booth and Quin.* — If that thou be'st a Roman *explained.* — *Quin.* — *Abbé le Blanc and David Garrick.* — *Scene between Amintor and Melantius.* — *Hector and Troilus.* — *Dorax and Sebastian.* — *Agamemnon and Menelaus.* — *The conclusion.*

Act II. Scene II.

Cæsar, Brutus, C. Ligarius, Antony, &c.

CÆSAR.

——— ——— Caius Ligarius,
Cæsar was ne'er so much your enemy
As that same ague which hath made you lean.

THERE is scarce any part of Cæsar's character so well understood by Shakspeare, as the great urbanity of his manners, and the ease and affability of his conversation. If Cæsar was the greatest soldier,

 he

he ſeems likewiſe to have been the beſt-bred man of all antiquity. In this ſhort ſcene his addreſs varies with the character of the perſon to whom he ſpeaks. The compliment he pays to Caius Ligarius is a happy mixture of politeneſs and humanity.

Act III. The ſenate.

The aſſaſſination of Cæſar.

C Æ S A R.

Et tu, Brute! ——

As Decimus Brutus was a great favourite of Cæſar, it is perhaps doubtful, whether *Et tu, Brute!* was addreſſed to him or Marcus Brutus; however it is univerſally underſtood to have been ſpoken to the latter.

C I N N A.

Liberty! freedom! — tyranny is dead!

The queſtion of Cæſar's death has long been agitated, between the abettors of abſolute monarchy, and the friends of a republican

lican form of government. The diſpute has been managed with as much eagerneſs, as if their different ſtate-eſtabliſhments were highly intereſted in the juſtification or condemnation of the act. Perhaps, after all, the deciſion of the diſpute may not affect the principles of either party.

The proper queſtion is, whether the ſtate of Rome gained or loſt by Cæſar's murder, not whether Cæſar deſerved to be put to death. What ſort of liberty did the aſſaſſins propoſe to eſtabliſh after they had killed him? The democratical power of the Republic, which I will preſume to ſay was the moſt eſſential to the welfare of the people, had long ſince been extinguiſhed, or at leaſt ſo diminiſhed that its efficacy was dwindled to almoſt nothing. The ſenate had ſeized into their hands the whole power of the ſtate; the people enjoyed no more than that ſmall pittance of freedom which their lords and maſters were willing to allow them.

But the conſcript fathers themſelves were controuled and kept in awe by a ſmall number of their own members, who, from time to time, ſeized upon all offices and honours of the ſtate, and diſtributed them amongſt their friends and followers. Thus was the ariſtocracy melted down into an oligarchy.

Since the murder of their two great tribunes, Tiberius and Caius Gracchus, the Romans had enjoyed nothing but the ſhadow of liberty. Theſe men loſt their lives in a generous attempt to reſcue the poor from the oppreſſion of the rich. After their deaths, the power of the tribune, an office created to protect the rights and privileges of the plebeians, became, by the chicanery and injuſtice of the ſenate, an engine of power to enſlave and impoveriſh the people. The domination of Sylla completed the deſtruction of the tribunitian authority. He not only deprived them of their rights of legiſlation, but he paſſed a decree, by which every man who had

ſerved

ſerved that office was rendered incapable of occupying any other. The triumvirate of Pompey, Cæſar, and Craſſus, ſucceeded in a very ſhort ſpace of time to the uſurped power of Sylla; and, during the interval between that and the dictatorſhip of Cæſar, hired mobs, riots, and tumults, formed to ſupport the illegal pretenſions of the ſeveral candidates for the offices of the ſtate, continually alarmed and diſturbed the peace of the city. The provinces were infamouſly oppreſſed by the proconſuls. Thoſe, whom we call Engliſh nabobs, are not ſaid to be more ſolicitous to accumulate immenſe riches, by plundering whole principalities, and robbing the princes of the Eaſt, than theſe Roman governors were eager to pillage the nations over whom they were ſent to preſide. They deprived them of every thing that was valuable, in money and plate, pictures, jewels, pearls, ſtatues, or any thing eſteemed an object of taſte or avarice. The plebeians were become the willing ſlaves of the patricians, who, to gain their votes and intereſt, fed them with largeſſes, and diverted them with ſhows at an exorbitant expence. The number of Roman citizens, who were proprietors of land when Cæſar was put to death, did not, by computation, amount to more than two thouſand.* And this is an evident proof of the oppreſſion and injuſtice of the ſenate, and the profligacy and corruption of all orders in the ſtate. Give us honours, titles, and emoluments, ſaid the great to the populace, and, in return, we will give you money and ſhows. *Panem et circenſes* was even then all that the free citizens of Rome deſired. And were theſe the men for whom the life of Cæſar was to be ſacrificed? We are told indeed, that the beſt and wiſeſt of the Romans approved of the murder of Cæſar. It is ſtrange that even experience ſhould not have convinced theſe Romans that liberty could not be a bleſſing to a mob of ſlaves. Cicero, one of the wiſeſt men in Rome, was perſecuted and expoſed to baniſhment

* Gibbon's Decline of the Roman Empire. Vol. III.

banifhment for faving his country from the defperate confpiracy of Cataline; nor would he, perhaps, have been freed from exile, if the two great kings of Rome, Pompey and Cæfar, had not been difgufted with their infamous tool Clodius.

In this diftracted ftate of Rome, at the clofe of the civil war, the only man, capable to eftablifh fome regular form of government, was Julius Cæfar. His abilities in the cabinet were as folid as his actions in the field were fplendid. The qualities of his mind were noble, generous, and humane; of all the Romans, who had drawn the fword againft their countrymen, he was acknowledged to have been the moft merciful.

It is impoffible to juftify the confpirators upon any reafonable principle: they had been obliged as far as men could be obliged, they had been taken in arms fighting againft Cæfar, for Pompey, not for the republic: they were reftored to their country and to the enjoyment of the honours of the

the ſtate; ſeveral of them had received employments from the hands of Cæſar. Antony's reproach in act V. of the play, that, when they were preparing their daggers for his throat, they cried, *all hail, Cæſar!* was juſt. For, in the daily intercourſe of friendſhip and reciprocation of mutual offices, to plot a man's death is the groſſeſt violation of thoſe ſocial bands which unite men together, that can poſſibly be deviſed. We may, with all the appearance of truth, conclude, that the conſpirators hated all tyranny but their own; ariſtocracy was the idol for which they fought and died; and that is, of all forms of government, the beſt ſuited to men of intolerant principles, and the moſt oppreſſive to the people. God forbid that England ſhould be ever governed by a houſe of lords! and this I do not ſay from a want of due reverence to that auguſt aſſembly.

Many cauſes concurred to render the people of Rome diſqualified to receive that liberty which Brutus and the conſpirators pretended

pretended to offer them. They no more resembled the Romans who lived during the free days of the Republic than the Ægyphan mob, in Dryden's play of Cleomenes King of Sparta, were like the Greeks, who endeavoured to inspire them with a sense of liberty; a word, says Dryden, which they pronounced so feebly, that they seemed afraid of its being heard. Rome was at that time a mart of slaves and slavery; we cannot suppose that the precincts of Rome contained less than 500000 slaves. Many of the great men had no less than 20000 in their retinue, most of them for pomp and ostentation. Luxury of all kinds was carried to excess. The great contention was, who should have the most magnificent houses in Rome, and villas out of it, with the richest and most costly furniture. They cased their houses with marble, and their doors were plated with gold. They had tables of gold and precious stones, and drinking-cups estimated at 2 or 3000l. Julius Cæsar lay on a golden bed with a purple

purple covering. They had candlesticks estimated at the salary of a tribune, 403*l.* 12*s.* 11*d.* their passion for plate, jewels, and all kind of precious stones, was insatiable. Julius Cæsar presented Servilia, Brutus's mother, with a pearl worth 48437*l.* 10*s.* The luxury of the table went in the same pace with all the rest; a Roman of those times would have fought more lustily for a mullus, a fish not weighing above two pounds, and supposed to be the same as our surmullet, than for the cause of liberty: they rose in price from 30*l.* to 60*l.* What shall we think of the humanity of a Roman senator who fed his lampreys with the flesh of his condemned slaves? and of a supper given to two great men by a friend, which cost him 1614*l.* 11*s.* 8*d.** One young gentleman, the son of a player, Æsopus, treated his guests with costly pearl; a pearl for every guest made into pearl-cordial. I shall

* An entertainment, without any previous notice, given by Lucullus to Pompey and Cicero. Arbuthnot on Coins.

ſhall mention another ſpecies of luxury which is yet unknown to a modern table, though perhaps a nabob of taſte may ſome-time hence think of introducing it as an improvement fit for his ſavoir-vivre company. The Romans weighed their fiſhes at table, and took a pleaſure in beholding them expire. The death of a mullus, with the variety and change of colours in its laſt moments, ſays Dr. Arbuthnot from Pliny, was reckoned one of the moſt entertaining ſpectacles in the world. And now, I hope, we ſhall hear no more of the wiſeſt and beſt men amongſt the Romans approving the aſſaſſination of Julius Cæſar.

From the great number of perſons on the ſtage, during the repreſentation of Cæſar's murder, much difficulty in the action may ariſe, unleſs great accuracy is obſerved in the direction of thoſe who are employed. The ſeveral conſpirators, preſſing with eagerneſs to have a ſhare in ſtabbing the victim, muſt be ſo regulated as to prevent confuſion. Cæſar's anxiety to fall with decen-

cy,

cy, by covering his body with his mantle, ſhould be in the actor's memory; nor ſhould the manager forget to have a figure of a ſtatue, ſuppoſed to reſemble that of Pompey; the poet expreſſly mentions Cæſar's falling at his great rival's feet, and ſprinkling his ſtatue with his blood.

Who acted the part of Julius Cæſar originally is not known, nor is it a matter of importance. But, ſoon after the junction of the king's and Duke of York's company, about the year 1682, this tragedy was in all its parts ſo acted as it never had been perhaps before, and certainly has not ſince: Betterton Brutus, Smith Caſſius, Mark Antony by Kynaſton, and Julius Cæſar by Goodman. Griffin, Mountfort, Williams, Gillow, Jevon, Underhill, and Leigh, all very eminent actors, thought it no diminution of their conſequence to play the inferior parts.

Goodman was a very handſome gay fellow, as well as a very conſiderable performer on the ſtage. But Goodman's paſſions

were

were ſtrong and his appetites larger than his very moderate income of about 30 or 40s. per week could ſatisfy. And, to procure ſuch pleaſures as he moſt delighted in, he was reduced, as Colley Cibber ſays, to try his fortune on the highway. Whether it was after the road-adventure, or before, that the Dutcheſs of Cleveland threw her amorous glances on Goodman is not clear from ſtage-hiſtory. But I ſhould rather think that it happened afterwards that he fell into the dutcheſs's good graces. For Goodman, long before his death, was ſo happy in his finances, that he acted only occaſionally, perhaps when his noble miſtreſs wiſhed to ſee him in a principal character; for Goodman uſed to ſay *he would not act Alexander the Great but when he was certain that his Dutcheſs would be in the boxes to ſee him perform.* Cibber relates, with great nonchalance, that Goodman entered into a plot to aſſaſſinate King William, he ſuppoſes from gratitude to James

James II. who had pardoned his robbery on the highway.

Julius Cæſar was, in the opinion of the elder Mills, the part in tragedy which his ſon William acted with moſt propriety. I remember to have ſeen him perform it; and, though he was in general a ſnip-ſnap ſpeaker, a manner which Mr Garrick very happily mimicked in the Rehearſal, when ſpeaking before Mills himſelf, yet in Cæſar he gave ſuch an idea of the part as Shakſpeare intended.

Scene continues.

ANTONY'S SERVANT.

So ſays my maſter Antony.

BRUTUS.

Thy maſter is a wiſe and valiant Roman,
I never thought him worſe.

That Antony was valiant, cannot be denied: his beſt praiſe is, that he was a good ſoldier; but that he was wiſe, which comprehends moral virtue, or it means nothing, is a ſentiment unworthy the mouth of Brutus.

Nor

Nor ſhould our author have drawn his favourite either ſo ignorant a judge, or ſo groſs a flatterer of the moſt abandoned follower of Cæſar's fortunes.

MARK ANTONY.

O mighty Cæſar, art thou fallen ſo low!

Wilks, who above fifty years ſince acted Mark Antony, as ſoon as he entered the ſtage, without taking any notice of the conſpirators, walked ſwiftly up to the dead body of Cæſar and knelt down; he pauſed ſome time before he ſpoke; and, after ſurveying the corpſe with manifeſt tokens of the deepeſt ſorrow, he addreſſed it in a moſt affecting and pathetic manner. A graceful dignity accompanied the action and deportment of this actor.

IDEM.

I do beſeech you, if you bear me hard.

That is, *if you owe me any ill will.*

This is a frequent mode of expreſſion with Shakſpeare, and occurs no leſs than three times in acts II. and III. of this play.

IDEM.

Friends! Romans! countrymen!

It has not, I believe, been hitherto obſerved by any of the commentators, that this admirable piece of oratory, ſo happily divided into exordium, narration, and peroration, is the ſole product of our author's genius, unaſſiſted by his conductor, Plutarch. The only hint, which he has borrowed from that writer, is Antony's ſhewing the dead body of Cæſar to the populace: it is compoſed of ſuch topics as were moſt conducive to the deſired effect. The artful pauſes and interruptions ſerve to increaſe the ſkill and power of the ſpeaker, and to rouſe, aſtoniſh, and inflame, the minds of the auditors. The Duke of Buckingham has very prudently preſerved almoſt the whole of Antony's oration as the author wrote it, though he has preſumed to alter every other ſcene in the play.

No orator ever met with ſo ample a reward for a ſingle oration as Antony did for this funeral harangue over the body of Cæſar. The Grecian orators had large ſums

ſums for their ſpeeches. Iſocrates received from Nicocles King of Cyprus, for one oration, no leſs a ſum than 3875*l.* and Demoſthenes obtained from Harpalus 4000*l.* for one day's ſilence. The ſum Antony paid for Cicero's head, an article that may well come into the account of eloquence, was 8072*l.* 18*s.* 4*d.* being ten times more than was offered for any other proſcribed perſon. † The Roman orators had frequently the cauſes of kings, provinces, and cities, to plead, and were paid according to the riches and generoſity of the employers. But Antony took care to be his own pay-maſter. He was indebted, March 15, the day on which Cæſar was murdered, to the amount of 322916*l.* 13*s.* 4*d.* which immenſe ſum, by the fraudulent management of Cæſar's papers, he diſcharged before the firſt of April following.*

The action of Wilks in Antony, from the beginning to the end of the oration, was

† Dr. Arbuthnot. * Cicero's 2d Philippic.

critically adapted to produce the intended consequences of the speaker. His address through the whole was easy and elegant; but his voice wanted that fulness and variety, requisite to impress the sentiments and pathos with which the speech abounds: besides, Wilks was apt to strike the syllables too forcibly as well as uniformly. Mr. Barry's fine person and pleasing manner were well adapted to Mark Antony, but his utterance in recitation was not sufficiently sonorous, nor his voice flexible enough, to express the full meaning of the author in the opening of the address. When roused by passion, Barry rose superior to all speakers. His close of the harangue was as warm and glowing as the beginning was cold and deficient.

The only man, in my memory, whose powers were perfectly suited to all parts of this celebrated harangue, was William Milward, who, from enjoying a full-toned and harmonious pipe, was frequently tempted to sacrifice sense to sound. On particular occasions,

occaſions, and in ſome parts, he was known to be a judicious and accurate ſpeaker. In Mark Antony he had every thing for him which nature could beſtow, perſon, look, voice; his action and addreſs were eaſy without art, and his deportment, though not abſolutely perfect, was far from ungraceful: he opened the preparatory part of the oration in a low but diſtinct and audible voice; for nothing can atone for the want of articulation; to be heard is the firſt leſſon the actor ſhould be maſter of; nor can I applaud the apology of Baron, the French Roſcius, who, on his opening Racine's Iphigenia in a whiſpering tone, when called upon by a ſpectator to ſpeak louder, replied, *if he did he ſhould not act in character.* Milward, I ſay, began low, and, by gradual progreſs, roſe to ſuch a height, as not only to inflame the populace on the ſtage, but to touch the audience with a kind of enthuſiaſtic rapture; when he uttered the following lines:

—— —— But were I Brutus,
And Brutus Antony, there were an Antony

Would ruffle up your ſpirits, and put a tongue
In every wound of Cæſar, that ſhould move
The ſtones of Rome to riſe and mutiny.

It is ſcarcely to be conceived with what acclamations of applauſe this was accompanied.

Act IV. Scene III.

Brutus and Caſſius.

BRUTUS.

Did not great Julius bleed for juſtice ſake?
What *villain* touch'd his body, that did ſtab,
And not for juſtice?

By the word *villain*, a reader, not upon his guard, might be induced to ſuppoſe that Brutus termed himſelf and the reſt of the conſpirators a band of aſſaſſins; but his meaning is, that the loweſt in rank amongſt them all was actuated, in the killing of Cæſar, with motives of humanity and juſtice, in ridding the world of a plunderer and a robber.

CASSIUS.

Brutus, *bay* not me.

The old editions read *baite*, but *bay* has a peculiar and adapted ſenſe here; *do not bark*

bark and ſnap at me, like a dog, with your biting language. *Baying* is likewiſe a term applied to a deer, who, when hard run, turns upon the hounds.

IDEM.

——— Abler than yourſelf
To make conditions.

Dr. Johnſon ſuppoſes this boaſt of Caſſius to be from a ſuperior knowledge to confer offices at his diſpoſal.

If this refers to Lucius Pella, it will not hold; for he was an officer of Brutus, according to Shakſpeare's original, Plutarch; but I think the author meant ſomething more than this, which is but a mean accompliſhment for one who ſtyles himſelf a better ſoldier than his brother officer; I imagine it refers to the whole art military, whoſe various operations he preſumes to underſtand much better than Brutus.

CASSIUS.

———What, durſt not tempt him?

BRUTUS.

For your life, you durft not.

In this laft line of Brutus, the actors, from time immemorial, have made a fmall alteration, which I fuppofe they imagined would convey the fentiment with ftronger emphafis, and make a deeper impreffion on their auditors. Brutus faid, inftead of

> For your *life*, you durft not,
> No, for your *foul*, you durft not.

It muft not be forgotten that both their tempers are wrought up to the higheft pitch; Caffius to extreme anger and rage, and Brutus to a very warm, though affumedly calm, refolution; their fwords are half drawn, and their hilts fhould meet and repel each other. Quin fpoke *No, for your foul*, &c. with a look of anger approaching to rage. Booth, on the contrary, looking ftedfaftly at Caffius, pronounced the words with firmnefs indeed, but not raifed much above a whifper, which had

had much greater weight with the ſpecta-tors, and produced a ſtronger effect, than the loudneſs of Quin.

CASSIUS.

——Within, a heart
Dearer than Plutus' mine, richer than gold;
If that thou *be'ſt a Roman*, take it forth.

If thou art a Roman of the old ſtamp, reſembling Lucius Junius Brutus, thy great anceſtor, rigidly virtuous and inflexibly ſevere, ſuch an one as never knew what it was to pardon the leaſt deviation from right, here is my breaſt, take out my heart. This ſeems to be the meaning of Caſſius's warm and paſſionate offer.

BRUTUS.

When I ſpoke this I was ill-temper'd too.

Here we diſcover the real cauſe of Brutus's ſeverity to his friend: his own diſtreſs of mind and ruffled temper produced the pointed and animated declamation againſt the mercenary behaviour of Caſſius. This is generally the caſe; when friends fall out, the cauſe for quarrel is often juſt, but the immediate incentive to anger often proceeds from

from ſomething that is remote from it. The mind of Brutus was diſturbed by private calamity, he had juſt received letters acquainting him with the death of his beloved Portia. Caſſius came in his way, and, by provoking a quarrel, brought on himſelf an acrimonious though juſt reprehenſion of his corrupt and venal conduct. Caſſius juſtly merited all the reproaches of his friend; in his government of Syria he was infamouſly rapacious and oppreſſive.

IDEM.

No man bears ſorrow better. —— Portia is dead!

Quin's look and tone of voice, in uttering *Portia is dead!* were extremely affecting: his expreſſive pauſe before he ſpoke fixed the audience in deep attention.

This ſcene between Brutus and Caſſius was the admiration of the age in which the author lived, and has maintained its important character to this hour. But, ſuch was the delicacy of a Frenchman, abbé le Blanc, who reſided a few years in this country and wrote ſome letters on our cuſtoms

cuſtoms and manners, that, in his account of Shakſpeare's Julius Cæſar, he acquaints his friend that the two great Roman generals upbraided each other in the language of porters; Garrick aſſured me that when he was in France he refuſed an invitation to meet this author, on account of his profanation of Shakſpeare.

I will not pretend to ſay that the quarrel between Amintor and Melantius, in the Maid's Tragedy, is an imitation of Shakſpeare; the time when that play was fiirſt acted is unknown, the merit of that compoſition is great, the paſſions are worked up from ſuch incidents as ariſe from the plot and the ſituation of the characters; it is impoſſible to read it without being ſtrongly affected; but, however meritorious it may be, it does not riſe to the ſupreme excellency of the ſcene between the *half-ſworded Romans*.

In Dryden's Troilus and Creſſida, the two brothers, Hector and Troilus, quarrel with great vehemence; the occaſion is intereſting. Love and honour never appeared to more advantage than in this animated

animated ſcene; the paſſions have their full vent, and the cloſe is pleaſingly affect-ing. Dryden has the entire merit of it, there being no hint of it in the original. But, when we have ſaid the beſt we can of it, ſtill art predominates over nature.

I am ſtill more pleaſed with the ſame author's interview between Mark Antony and Ventidius, where the honeſt hardy veteran ſtrives to rouſe his emperor and friend from his indolence and diſpondence, and awaken him to a ſenſe of honour. The combat between conſcious ſhame and acknowledgment of error is nobly fought, nor do I think any thing in all Dryden's plays ſo truly dramatic as this. Had ſuch a maſterly ſcene, inſtead of being placed in the firſt, been reſerved to the fourth or fifth act, All for Love would have challenged immortality; but, not being ſupported by any thing equal in the ſucceeding parts of the play, it is now generally neglected.

But Dryden valued himſelf more highly on the reconciliation-ſcene between Dorax and Sebaſtian in the play of that name;

and

and I believe that the tragedy was written for the ſake of the ſentiments introduced in it. But the upbraidings of Dorax to his royal maſter are coarſe, indecent, and brutal. Who can be intereſted greatly for a man who turns a rebel to his prince and an apoſtate to his faith, becauſe a rival-courtier is preferred to him? Many elevated thoughts with ſome warm conflicts of paſſion, we muſt allow, the ſcene does not want. But there is in it too much ſwell of diction, and too great parade and pomp of action; nature is ſtifled by art, and art too diſcernible.

The only ſcene which in my opinion can be compared with that of Shakſpeare's Brutus and Caſſius, for natural dialogue and truth of paſſion, is that admirable one between Agamemnon and Menelaus in the Iphigenia in Aulis, of Euripides. The ſtory is well known. The Grecian fleet is detained at Aulis by contrary winds: Calchas declares Diana will not grant a fair wind unleſs the general's daughter is ſacrificed to her. Agamemnon ſends for Iphigenia,

genia, under the pretence of matching her to Achilles; but afterwards, in the diſtraction of paternal feelings, he diſpatches a truſty meſſenger to forbid her coming. Menelaus meets the ſervant and forces the letter from him. He upbraids his brother in the ſharpeſt terms for his duplicity; the quarrel proceeds to extremity; when, on a ſudden, a meſſenger enters, and acquaints Agamemnon that Clytemneſtra and Iphigenia are juſt arrived. The diſtreſs of the father rouſes all the affection of Menelaus, who, after ſilently contemplating the ſufferings of his unhappy brother, approaches him with unſpeakable tenderneſs, and begs his hand.

Αδελφε, δος μοι δεξιας της σης θιγειν.

The laſt act of Julius Cæſar has nothing either in action or ſentiment that is very remarkable. Mark Antony's character of Brutus has been often quoted and much celebrated.

This was the nobleſt Roman of them all:
All the conſpirators, ſave only he,

Did

Did that they did in envy of great Cæſar;
He only, in a general good to all, made one of them:
His life was gentle, and the elements
So mix'd in him, that nature might ſtand up
And ſay to all the world, this was a-man.*

Brutus was extremely unfit to be a ring-leader in a conſpiracy; his amiable and gentle ſpirit could not encounter the rough and thorny buſineſs neceſſary to bring about a revolution in the ſtate. The times he lived in were too degenerate and corrupt for ſo mild a reformer. His great anceſtor, Lucius Junius Brutus, could not have effected, in the days of Cæſar, what his hardy virtue and perſevering ſpirit ſo nobly accompliſhed in an age undebauched by luxury.

Julius Cæſar, though now laid aſide and almoſt forgotten, was long the favourite of an Engliſh audience; though the

* It muſt be confeſſed that Brutus, after the battle of Pharſalia, too haſtily forſook the cauſe he had eſpouſed: he not only made his peace immediately with Cæſar; but, by his advice, the conqueror determined to follow Pompey into Ægypt.

the ſubject did not invite Shakſpeare to aſcend *the brighteſt heaven of his invention*, though it afforded no place for magical inchantment, nor any ſtrong and powerful exhibition of the tumultuous or ſofter paſſions of the heart, yet the poet has kept faithfully to the object he had in view. Roman manners and characters are repreſented with great energy and gravity of ſentiment, with ſuperior grace and dignity of action. The hot and ſelfiſh Caſſius is finely contraſted with the philoſophic and generous Brutus. The art of Mark Antony is ſkilfully unfolded; his oration over the dead body of Cæſar is ſuch a maſterpiece of eloquence as is not to be matched in any play antient or modern.

For a more complete view of the merits of this tragedy, I muſt refer my reader to the judicious remarks of the accompliſhed Mrs. Montague, in her excellent Eſſay on the Genius and Writings of Shakſpeare.

King Lear.

CHAPTER XXXI.

Tragedy of Lear *ſuppoſed not to be originally much admired. — Fewer editions of it than many of Shakſpeare's other plays. — Leonard Diggs. — Downs.* — Lear *not often acted in its priſtine ſtate. — Tate's vanity. — Mr. Colman's Lear. — Tate's ſcenes of Edgar and Cordelia. — Addiſon's and Richardſon's judgement of Lear's cataſtrophe. — Dr. Johnſon. — Count Ugolino. — Sir Joſhua Reynolds. — Garrick. — Lear's fool. — Woodward.*— Paſſage *explained.— Scene judiciouſly reſtored by Mr. Colman. — The baſtard. — Savage. — His poem.— Mr. Steevens, Dr. Warburton, and Vanini.* — Unſtate myſelf *explained.* — Old fools are babes, &c. *diſcuſſed. — Character of the gentleman-uſher.* — Lear *not a favourite*

 of

of the audience in former times.— Booth.— Wilks, Mrs. Booth, and Boheme. — Macklin's opinion of Boheme's Lear. — *His person, voice, and manner. — Print to Mariamne. — Mrs. Boheme. — Quin's Lear. — Booth in uttering Lear's curſe inferior to Garrick. — Powell's Lear. — Meaning of ſome paſſages. —* Sop of moon-ſhine. — Barber-monger. — Enormous ſtate, &c. — *The ſuperior worth of Kent's character. — Winſtone, Branſby. — Sparks. — Mr. Horne Tooke. — Clarke.— Edgar's diſguiſe. — Tricks of old impoſtors. — Garrick's happy reſtoration of a paſſage.* — Tender-hefted *explained. — Worthleſs Penſioners.*

NOTWITHSTANDING the tragedy of King Lear is univerſally eſteemed to be one of Shakſpeare's nobleſt productions, I cannot help ſuſpecting that it was not held in equal regard, or at leaſt not ſo much followed, when firſt brought on the ſtage, as many other of our author's pieces which

which are not ſuperior to it in merit. Mr. Steevens ſpeaks only of two editions of Lear in quarto, prior to the edition of our author's works in folio, 1623. Many of his leſs perfect efforts were given to the public five or ſix times before the publication of the folio. None of his contemporaries, who have come down to us, have mentioned this maſterpiece of plot, paſſion, and moral. If any traces of that kind could have been found, the accurate Mr. Malone would have inſerted them in his new-raiſed monument to the memory of Shakſpeare, the large ſupplement to his works. Leonard Diggs, in a rapturous viſion, propheſied eternity to our author in the following lines prefixed to the *edition of Hemnings and Condell:*

——— ——— This book,
When braſs and marble fade, ſhall make thee look
Freſh to all ages, when poſterity
Shall lothe what's new, think all is prodigy
That is not Shakſpeare's. ———

And, in another copy of verſes, prefixed to his poems, in which the ſame author has pointed out ſix or ſeven of his principal characters, he has taken no notice of Lear: however, as he has likewiſe omitted others of great importance, I ſhall not inſiſt upon an argument ſo very uncertain. Downs, in his Roſcius Anglicanus, will enable me to go farther, and upon ſafer ground. He tells us, that, about the year 1663, King Lear was acted, at the Duke's Theatre, *as Shakſpeare wrote it*. The principal character was doubtleſs repreſented by Betterton, he being at the head of the company. But Downs is ſilent as to the effect produced by this play; though he enlarges ſomewhat upon the Othello of Hart, and more upon the Hamlet and Henry VIII. of Betterton. The ſucceſs of Macbeth is alſo particularized by this ſtage-hiſtorian. It ſhould ſeem then that even the action of a Betterton could not ſupport a play, with a cataſtrophe ſo ſhocking and terrible to human nature.

That Lear in its priſtine ſtate was not often repreſented, ſoon after the reſtoration, we may then reaſonably infer from Downs: and,

and, till Tate produced his alteration of this play, it had to all appearance been laid aside and neglected as unprofitable to the players. Tate himself seems to have been a stranger to its merit till he had examined it, and found a new-discovered treasure of jewels unstrung and unpolished, as he ostentatiously informs us. Though the man is to be laughed at for his vanity, in pretending to mend Shakspeare, and, especially for claiming the play as his own, which he does in the title to one of his pieces; yet, it must be confessed, that, weak as he is, he has rescued the play from that oblivion to which the actors had consigned it.

Mr. Colman has within these few years printed an altered Lear of his own, with many judicious restorations from the original copy. I heartily wish he had not taken such a dislike to the passion of Edgar for Cordelia; he would have rescued that love-plan, which I think a good one, from meaner hands, and given a new lustre to the play. Even Mr. Colman was, after mature deliberation, obliged to make Lear end happily. The lovers of Cordelia in the old play do not ſurely make a more reſpectable figure than Edgar; Burgundy is juſt ſhewn to be deſpiſed. The King of France too had ſojourned long in the court of Lear, and, though he diſplays a generous concern for Cordelia's unfortunate ſituation, he ſeems to have made no previous declaration of his paſſion to her, the lady likewiſe manifeſts no other regard for him than giving her hand and complying with her deſtiny. The paſſion of Edgar and Cordelia is happily imagined; it ſtrongly connects the main plot of the play and renders it more intereſting to the ſpectators; without this, and the conſequent happy cataſtrophe, the alteration of Lear would have been of little worth; beſides, after thoſe turbulent ſcenes of reſentment, violence, diſobedience, ingratitude, and rage, between Lear and his two eldeſt daughters, with the king's conſequent agony and diſtraction, the unexpected interview of Cordelia

delia and Edgar in act III. gives a pause of relief to the harassed and distressed minds of the audience. It is a gleam of sunshine and a promise of fair weather in the midst of storm and tempest. I have seen this play represented twenty or thirty times, yet I can truly affirm that the spectators always dismissed the two lovers with the most rapturous applause. Besides, it should be observed, that, without such an intervention as this, the action of the play would fall too heavily upon Lear, who stands in need of all the relief which the conduct of the fable can afford him. As a writer of plays, a scholar, and critic, I will not compare Mr. Garrick to Mr. Colman; as a man experienced in the conduct of a theatre, and one who well understood what would best please the taste of an audience, I must suppose him equal if not superior to all competition. He long considered the advantages and disadvantages which might flow from the exclusion or the retaining the scenes of Tate in question; and, after well-weighed

 reflection,

reflection, he thought proper to preserve the greatest part of them.

The judgement of Addison, who has flatly given his opinion against Tate's alteration of the catastrophe, is not to be implicitly relied on. In an essay or two in the Spectator, concerning dramatic writing and poetical justice, this excellent author has taken the melancholy side of the question, and is in my opinion too great an advocate for the poisoned bowl and the bloody dagger.

The pathetic Richardson, in his Clarissa, has embraced Addison's opinion, relative to the catastrophe of Lear. I shall beg leave to oppose to these writers the judgement of one, whose superiority in critical knowledge is universally allowed: Dr. Johnson observes, that a play, in which the wicked prosper and the virtuous miscarry, may doubtless be good, because it is a just representation of the common events of human life; but since, says this writer, all reasonable beings naturally love justice, I

cannot

cannot eafily be perfuaded, that the obfervation of juftice makes a play worfe, or that, if other excellences are equal, the audience will not always rife better pleafed from the final triumph of perfecuted virtue. He proceeds to fay that, in the prefent cafe, the public has decided; Cordelia, from the time of Tate, has always retired with victory and felicity. He farther fays, that, many years ago, he was fo fhocked by Cordelia's death, that he knows not whether he ever endured to read again the laft fcenes of the play till he undertook to revife them as an editor. *Johnfon and Steevens's Shakfpeare*, vol IX. p. 566. *laft edition.*

If thefe fcenes are really fo afflicting to a mind of fenfibility in the clofet, what would they produce in action? What exquifite grief and unutterable horror would fuch a painter as Garrick, in the laft fcene of the play, have raifed in the breaft of a fpectator? Who can endure to look for any confiderable time at the agonizing woe in the countenance of Count Ugolino, drawn

drawn by the inimitable pencil of Reynolds? But were you to produce that ſubject on the ſtage, in action, none but a heart of marble could ſuſtain it. The cataſtrophes of Shakſpeare and Tate are ſtrongly marked in the following lines, ſpoken by Edgar to Albany, in the laſt act of the play.

This would have ſeem'd a period
To ſuch as love not ſorrow.

That is, *ſuch as do not love to feed upon melancholy*.

——— But another,
To amplify too much, would make much more,
And top extremity.

For ſuch people the cup of bitterneſs muſt overflow to pleaſe them.

The cruel never ſhed tears, it is true, but to be continually weeping is more than humanity can bear. The ſlaughter of characters in the laſt act of the old Lear too much reſembles the concluſion of Tom Thumb; for no man of any conſequence is left alive except Albany and Edgar.

It was once in contemplation with Mr. Garrick to reſtore the part of the fool, which

which he designed for Woodward, who promised to be very chaste in his colouring, and not to counteract the agonies of Lear: but the manager would not hazard so bold an attempt; he feared, with Mr. Colman, that the feelings of Lear would derive no advantage from the buffooneries of the parti-coloured jester.*

FRANCE.

——— Sure her offence
Must be of such unnatural degree
That monsters it; or your fore-vouch'd affection
Fall into taint.

The King of France does by no means charge Lear with vouching affection for Cordelia which he did not feel, as Dr. Johnson seems to interpret the passage: his meaning is, that either she, who was so lately your darling and your dearest child, must have committed some enormous offence, or you must be censured for placing your affections upon one who did not possess

* In all probability, Nokes, *whose face was a comedy*, acted the Fool with Betterton's Lear: if so, we may guess the consequence.

ſeſs thoſe qualities which your fondneſs has attributed to her.

After the King has returned with Burgundy and France, and a ſhort converſation between Cordelia and her two elder ſiſters has taken place, Shakſpeare thought proper to prepare the audience for the outrageous acts of diſobedience and cruelty, committed by Goneril and Regan, againſt their father, in a ſhort ſcene, wherein the tempers of the two ladies are unfolded, and their intention to be conjunct in the treatment of their father declared; this neceſſary dialogue Mr. Colman has judiciouſly preſerved, but it eſcaped the diligence of Mr. Garrick.

Scene II. Edmund's ſoliloquy.

EDMUND.

Thou, Nature, art my goddeſs!
——— Why *baſtard?* wherefore *baſe?*
Who, in the luſty ſtealth of nature, take
More compoſition and fierce quality
Than doth within a dull, ſtale, tir'd, bed

Go

Go to the creating of a whole tribe of fops,
Got 'tween asleep and wake!

Some of the warmest and most poetical lines, in Savage's poem of the Bastard, are little more than a paraphrase of Edmund's soliloquy.

Blest be the bastard's birth, through won'drous ways
He shines excentric like the comet's blaze;
No sickly fruit of faint compliance he,
He's stamp'd in nature's mint with extacy;
He lives to build, not boast, a generous race,
No tenth transmitter of a foolish face,
He kindling from within requires no flame,
He glories in a bastard's glowing name.

In the Revenger's Tragedy, first printed in 1607, Spurio, the Bastard, says,

——— Adultery is my nature;
Faith, if the truth were known, I was begot
After some gluttonous dinner, some stirring dish
Was my first father, when deep healths went round,
And ladies cheeks were painted red with wine,
Their tongues, as short and nimble as their heels,
Uttering words sweet and thick.*

Mr. Steevens justly refutes Dr. Warburton's opinion of Shakspeare's intending to make

* Vide Mr. Reed's accurate edition of Dodsley's old plays, vol IV.

make Edmund a confirmed atheiſt. The ſtrange wiſh of Vanini, that he had been born a baſtard, which the doctor has quoted in his notes on Edmund's ſpeech of baſtardy, and contains ſomething very like Shakſpeare, is brought to prove the divinity of our poet's genius, which foretold (as it were) what ſuch an atheiſt as Vanini would ſay. With ſubmiſſion, this is all gratis dictum. The reader of this ſoliloquy may eaſily perceive that Edmund ſufficiently feels the diſgrace of illegitimacy, but that he is willing to make the beſt of it, and affects to embrace that with a hearty good-will, which he would fain, if in his power, throw aſide; and this is human nature: how many affect to be fond of, or laugh at, a blemiſh of birth, or an accident of time, which they cannot avoid? Shakſpeare makes Richard the Third talk with unconcern of his crooked back and bandy legs, and take pleaſure in *deſcanting on his own deformity*.

GLOSTER.

GLOSTER.

I would *unſtate* myſelf to be in a due reſolution.

I cannot be convinced that any of the commentators have given a proper ſolution of the word *unſtate*.

The Earl, between his regard for a ſon whom he tenderly loves, and the evidence produced by Edmund of his diſobedience and undutiful behaviour, is in a ſtate of perplexity and the moſt doubtful anxiety. Therefore he intreats Edmund to make uſe of all his art and contrivance to diſcover the real diſpoſition of Edgar. To obtain the knowledge of this truth he makes uſe of an expreſſion which is of the ſame import with one often uſed upon ſimilar, or indeed ſlighter, occaſions. "To know the truth "of this or that matter, I would give all "I am worth in the world; for then I ſhall "know what to do." And this is, I think, the true meaning of *unſtate myſelf to be in a due reſolution*.

Scene

Scene III.

GONERIL.

—— Now, by my life,
Old fools are babes again, and muſt be us'd
With checks, as flatteries, when they are ſeen, abus'd.

Two notes of ſome length are employed upon this paſſage by Dr. Warburton and Dr. Johnſon, neither of which is ſatisfactory: the laſt commentator indeed ſeems to imagine that the author did not think theſe lines worth his correcting, and for that reaſon threw them away: but, this is getting rid of a difficulty at the expence of the poet. I think the following explanation will get ſomething like ſenſe out of theſe obſcure lines.

Old people, ſays Goneril, when turned to dotage, muſt be managed with the ſame controul, and checked in the ſame manner we do groſs flatterers, who overſhoot the mark. The firſt are peeviſh and troubleſome from decay of their faculties, and the others are offenſive from their want of diſcretion.

Act

Act I. Scene IV.

Enter Steward, or Oſwald.

The Steward is a neceſſary implement employed by the poet to carry on the plot: I have ſeen it acted by ſeveral eminent players, Yates, Shuter, King, Dodd, &c. but the character is ſo diſtaſteful, and by the comedians falſely ſuppoſed to be unimportant, that all of them, of any note, no ſooner get into the part but they grow tired and withdraw from it. He generally enters the ſtage in a careleſs diſengaged manner, humming a tune, as if on purpoſe to give umbrage to the King by his neglect of him. Vernon was impudently negligent and characteriſtically provoking in Oſwald; however he grew too great for the part; and it is now acted by an inferior player.

STEWARD.

I'll not be ſtruck, my lord!

KENT.

Nor tript neither, you *baſe foot-ball player.*

By this low term of *baſe foot-ball player,* Kent means, that *he reſembles a fellow,*

 who,

who, in endeavouring to kick the bladder or ball, miſſes his aim and tumbles down.

GONERIL.

——— Put it on
By your allowance.

Encourage it by your authority.

IDEM.

———More like a tavern, or a brothel,
Than a grac'd palace.

More reſembling a houſe of diſorderly entertainment than the reſidence of a prince, where all things ſhould be managed with order, grace, and decorum.

LEAR.

Hear, nature, dear goddeſs, hear a father!

Much has been ſaid by Downs, by the Tatler, by Cibber, and others, of Betterton's uncommon powers of action and utterance in ſeveral of Shakſpeare's principal parts, particularly Hamlet, Macbeth, Othello, and Brutus, but no writer has taken notice of his exhibition of Lear; a part of equal conſequence, and requiring as perfect ſkill in the player as any of them. I am almoſt tempted to believe that this tragedy, notwithſtanding

withſtanding that Tate's alterations were approved, was not in an ſuch equal degree of favour, with the public, as Hamlet, Othello, and many other of our poet's dramas. The Spectators, when they were firſt publiſhed, contained theatrical advertiſements, but no Lear is, I believe, to be found amongſt them; had it been a favourite tragedy, Wilks, after the death of Betterton, would, in all probability, have ſeized Lear for his friend John Mills; and this would have ſerved the double purpoſe of elevating his favourite and of depreſſing Booth, whoſe pretenſions to the character were more juſt. It is in vain, therefore, to talk of Betterton's Lear, for we know nothing of it. After Booth became Wilks's brother-manager he could then talk to him as an equal, and claim ſuch parts as were due to his merit: and, ſometime after he had acquired a ſhare in the patent, he undertook the repreſentation of Lear, and was much admired in it. His Cordelia was Mrs. Booth; ſhe was well ſuited, by the agreableneſs of her perſon, her voice, and manner of ſpeaking, to ſeveral of the ſoft and gentler females, ſuch as Ophelia in Hamlet, and Selima in Tamerlane: however, I think ſhe was rather a cold actreſs in tragedy; in comedy ſhe diſplayed a pleaſing vivacity and elegant deportment, that charmed the public long; in the Harriet of Etherege's Sir Fopling Flutter ſhe ſang ſome of the London cries very agreeably; but her chief excellence conſiſted in a graceful manner of dancing. It was ſaid of Booth, who would ſometimes act lazily, that Lear was one of thoſe parts which he never ſlighted. But, however excellent Booth's performance of this character was, he had no mean competitor in a young actor, who, from ſmall beginnings, roſe to a very high degree of eſtimation with the public.

Antony Boheme was firſt taken notice of at ſome booth, either in Bartholomew or Southwark fair, for a manner of ſpeaking and acting ſuperior to his ſituation. Mr. Rich employed him firſt at a very low ſalary, but his great merit ſoon increaſed his

his income. As he was an original actor and not an auricular imitator, his manner of acting Lear was very different from that of Booth. Mr. Macklin ſpeaks of Boheme's ſtage-abilities with great approbation. To his Lear he gave a trait, he ſays, of the antique. In his perſon he was tall, his features were expreſſive, with ſomething of the venerable caſt, which gave force and authority to the various ſituations and paſſions of the character; the tones of his voice very equally powerful and harmonious, and his whole action ſuited to the age and feelings of Lear. I never ſaw a portrait of this very valuable comedian. But there is an engraving to the ſecond edition of Mariamne, by Vertue, from a drawing of his own, which exhibited ſome of the principal characters in that tragedy, and not unlike the actors who repreſented them, particularly Herod and Mariamne by Boheme and Mrs. Seymour. The figure and countenance of Boheme appears majeſtic and expreſſive. Quin, who had acted Gloſter in the ſame play many years with great approbation of the public, was after the death of Boheme, perſuaded to try his abilities in Lear. No leſs than twenty-two rehearſals were demanded by him; but he, being at that time young and diſſipated, attended only two of them. He fell infinitely ſhort of his predeceſſor in almoſt every ſcene of Lear. Quin felt neither the tender nor the violent emotions of the ſoul, and therefore ſhould not have hazarded his reputation in a part for which nature unfitted him. However, as he was a man of undeniable merit and an excellent ſpeaker, he did not ſo entirely offend as to throw himſelf out of public favour. Booth, who was an actor of genius, and though a profeſſed admirer of Betterton almoſt to idolatry, had too much judgement to copy or ſervilely imitate his action. He has been known to read a ſcene in a part, acted by Betterton, in that great actor's mannner, to the admiration of his hearers; but, when aſked why he would not ſo repreſent a character throughout, his conſtant anſwer was, that it was too much

much for him. He ſtole what he could from his great exemplar, and fitted it to his own powers and manner, juſt as that agreeable actor, William Powell, did by Garrick. In uttering the imprecation on Goneril, Booth was more rapid than Garrick, his fire was ardent and his feelings were remarkably energetic, but they were not attended with thoſe ſtrugglings of parental affection, and thoſe powerful emotions of conflicting paſſions, ſo viſible in every look, action, and attitude, of our great Roſcius. I have heard certain critics complain, that, in pronouncing this denunciation, Garrick was too deliberate, and not ſo quick in the emiſſion of his words as he ought to have been; that he did not yield to that impetuoſity which his particular ſituation required. But we ſhould reflect, that Lear is not agitated by one paſſion only, that he is not moved by rage, by grief, and indignation, ſingly, but by a tumultuous combination of them all together, where all claim to be heard at once, and where one naturally interrupts the progreſs of the other. Beſides, the lines are ſo full of rich and diſtinct matter, that few men can roll them off with any degree of ſwiftneſs. Shakſpeare, we ſhould conſider, too, wrote them for the mouth of one who was to aſſume the action of an old man of fourſcore, for a father as well as a monarch, in whom the moſt bitter execrations are accompanied with extreme anguiſh, with deep ſighs, and involuntary tears. Garrick rendered the curſe ſo terribly affecting to the audience, that, during his utterance of it, they ſeemed to ſhrink from it as from a blaſt of lightning. His preparation for it was extremely affecting; his throwing away his crutch, kneeling on one knee, claſping his hands together, and lifting his eyes towards heaven, preſented a picture worthy the pencil of a Raphael.

In Barry's perſonating Lear, his figure was dignified and venerable; his manner of ſpeaking this celebrated imprecation was impreſſive; but his voice wanted that pow-

er

er and flexibility which varied paſſion requires. His pauſes and broken interruptions of ſpeech, of which he was extremely enamoured, ſometimes to a degree of impropriety, were at times too inartificially repeated; nor did he give that terror to the whole which the great poet intended ſhould predominate.

Powell's king Lear ought not to be forgotten, it was a fair promiſe of ſomething great in future. He had about him the bloſſoms of an excellent actor; many ſcenes of the choleric king were well adapted to his fine conceptions of the paſſions, and eſpecially thoſe of the ſofter kind. Had he lived till now we ſhould not have regretted quite ſo much the loſs of our great tragic actors, Garrick and Barry.

Dr. Franklin thinks nothing can exceed the bitterneſs of OEdipus's execration of his two ſons, except perhaps the curſe of Lear on his daughter: from the following extract the reader may perhaps determine.

OEDIPUS.

——— Meantime, thou worſt,
Thou moſt abandon'd, of the ſons of men,

Be

Be gone away, and with thee bear this curſe
Which here I do pronounce: To Argos ne'er
May'ſt thou return! never may Thebes be thine!
Soon may'ſt thou periſh by a brother's hand!
Slaying the ſlayer! May dark Erebus
Receive them both! And now on you I call,
Ye goddeſſes rever'd! and thou, O Mars!
Thou, who haſt rais'd the bitter ſtrife between
My impious ſons, bear witneſs to my words!

Franklin's tranſlation of Sophocles's
Œdipus Coloneus.

In Lear's curſe there are two or three paſſages on which I ſhall offer ſomething.

LEAR.

Create her *child of ſpleen!*

That is, *malicious* and *diſobedient.*

IDEM.

——— That it may live
And prove a thwart diſnatur'd torment to her!

Something like this is to be found in the execration pronounced on ſacrilegious perſons amongſt the Greeks.

IDEM.

The *untented* woundings of a father's curſe
Pierce every ſenſe about thee!

The

The incurable execrations of a parent. The curſes of parents amongſt the antients were greatly dreaded, for they were ſuppoſed to be always fulfilled.

Act II.

EDMUND.

In cunning I muſt draw my ſword upon you.

I muſt ſeem to be your enemy, though I am not, leſt my father ſhould ſuſpect me to be in confederacy with you.

Scene VI.

REGAN.

Threading dark night.

This is a metaphor plainly borrowed from the threading of a needle. Our buſineſs, ſays Regan, is of ſuch importance, that it obliges us to travel by night, though it be as difficult to keep the right road in darkneſs as it is to hit the eye of a needle without a ſteady hand and a proper thread. This I think is our author's meaning.

Kent

Kent and Oſwald.

This incident of a quarrel between the two meſſengers from Lear and Goneril is admirably contrived to advance the buſineſs or plot of the play, it contributes to open the character of Regan more at large, and of Cornwall, who was hitherto unknown: it alſo prepares the reader for the grand ſcene of terror which concludes act II.

KENT.

I'll make a ſop of the moonſhine of you.

This was, in all probability, in Shakſpeare's days, a proverbial expreſſion. A mouthful of moonſhine was firſt introduced, I believe, into converſation by a member of the Iriſh parliament, ſoon after the revolution: this ſignifies *a bite at a ſhadow:* by the other, Kent means, that, *by the help of the moon, he will diſpatch him as quickly as he would eat a morſel of bread.*

IDEM.

You *neat* ſlave!

Mr.

Mr. Steevens has interpreted the word *neat* very juſtly by *finical*, which is a certain impertinence in dreſs and behaviour.

Neatneſs itſelf impertinent in him. POPE.

This is farther explained above by glaſs-gazing, and this too will help us to the meaning, if I miſtake not, of barber-monger, a fellow, whoſe hair is powdered and curled moſt exactly; what the French term *bien poudré*. So Mark Antony, when moſt completely prepared by dreſs to meet Cleopatra, is ſaid by Ænobarbus to be *barber'd all o'er*.

IDEM.

Thou whoreſon zed, thou unneceſſary letter.

Unneceſſary becauſe compounded of two other letters, *S*, *D*. Grammarians tell us the Doric Zeta is compoſed of theſe two letters.

IDEM.

Spare my grey beard, you *wag-tail*.

This word is of the ſame ſignification, I believe, as *bob-tail*, which is a cant term for

an

an eunuch or any impotent perſon. Shakſpeare makes this Oſwald an abſtract of all vices of the worſt kind, and perhaps he might mean the ſame thing as Juvenal does by the word *ceventem*.

—— Ego te *ceventem*, Sexte, verebor?
Juvenal, Sat. II.

REGAN.

These kind of knaves I know, which in their plainneſs
Harbour more craft and more corrupter ends
Than twenty ſilly ducking obſervants
Who ſtretch their duties nicely.

The fellow who affects the character of a plain downright man, who calls himſelf John Blunt, is more to be guarded againſt than the ſupple flatterer, who watches your looks to ſhew his ready obedience to your commands, and ſtretches his duty to a ridiculous exceſs to gain ſome reward for his pains.

Regan admits that both characters are worthleſs, but the latter, ſhe ſays, is far leſs dangerous than the former.

KENT.

——None of theſe rogues and cowards,
But Ajax is their ſport.

The

The brave plain honeſt man is the butt of the moſt deſpicable wretches.

IDEM.

——— Nothing almoſt ſees miracles
But miſery. ——— ———

That is, misfortune is induſtrious, and is ever on the watch, and diſcovers that, to which buſy proſperity cannot attend.

KENT [READING A LETTER.]

——— And ſhall find time,
From this *enormous ſtate* — ſeeking to give
Remedies. ——— ———

Kent, upon looking on the letter from Cordelia, ſays that ſhe has been informed of his courſe. Cordelia could have poſſibly learned no more, than that the generous Kent had diſguiſed himſelf to ſerve at all hazards his injured maſter, together with the inſolent behaviour of Goneril to her father. Regan had not as yet ſeen Lear; conſequently her conduct could not be arraigned by the name of *enormous rule*, as Mr. Steevens imagines; nor could Cordelia know

know what paſſed in this laſt ſcene. Dr. Johnſon has rightly interpreted the word *enormous* by *ſomething unwonted and out of rule.* Cordelia plainly intimates, that, as ſoon as ſhe could diſburthen herſelf from that weight of pomp and ceremony which attended her new dignity of queen of France, ſhe would immediately endeavour to correct thoſe evils which the ungrateful and wicked conduct of Goneril had brought upon her father.

It is the peculiar privilege of Shakſpeare to draw characters of the moſt ſingular form, and ſuch as, though acknowledged to come from nature's mint, had never entered into the mind of any other writer, antient or modern. This man combined, in his imagination, all the poſſibilities of human action with all the varieties of ſituation and paſſion. It is in this wonderful creative faculty that he excels all dramatic writers. He alone ſeems to have diſcerned how far the exerciſe of the nobleſt qualities of the mind could and ought to proceed.

ceed. The generoſity of Kent is not to be matched in any other drama, antient or modern. The man who has the courage, in the face of a court, to reprove his prince for an act of folly, violence, and injuſtice, after being condemned by him to perpetual baniſhment for his honeſt freedom, apprehenſive leſt ſome ill conſequences ſhould attend his maſter's raſh conduct, aſſumes a mean diſguiſe with no other view than to ſerve him in his utmoſt need, to wait upon him as his menial ſervant, and to do him all ſervile offices his neceſſities ſhould require. No man will think ſo meanly of human nature as not to acknowledge that virtue ſo diſintereſted is the growth of humanity. None but a Shakſpeare ever conceived ſo noble an example of perſiſting goodneſs and generous fidelity.

The name of the comedian who originally repreſented Kent is as much unknown as that of any other early performer in the tragedy. Winſtone, a man of rather large bulk, harſh features, and a rough loud voice,

 who,

who, about thirty years ſince, acted Kent when Garrick was the Lear, had a good deal of that manly boldneſs which is one ſtriking trait of the part, more eſpecially when he firſt puts on the diſguiſe; but he could not equally aſſume the generous feelings of the ſympathizing friend, who ſuffered more in his mind than did his unhappy and diſtreſſed old maſter. Branſby, his ſucceſſor, more happily expreſſed that affectionate humanity which is the brighteſt part of Kent's character. Branſby was ſpirited without being boiſterous, and blunt without vulgarity. Luke Sparks had likewiſe conſiderable merit in this part. Luke, though no ſcholar, was a man of ſtrong intelligence, and knew how to take poſſeſſion of a character, but he ſometimes gave too much hardneſs to his manner, his colouring was coarſe though his outline was generally exact. I am pleaſed to find that no actor has copied the particular ſtep of Sparks, which he too often enlarged into a ſtrut. Sparks acquired a competent fortune, though,

I

I believe, not entirely from acting. He retired from the ſtage about twenty years ſince, and lived at Brentford. He died about ſixteen years ago; and, with his almoſt dying breath, begged that the funeral ſervice might be pronounced over him by Mr. Horne, now Mr. Horne-Tooke. Mr. Clarke is at preſent a very reſpectable repreſenter of Kent's honeſt fervour and generous fidelity.

Scene III.

EDGAR, [SOLUS.]

—— My face I will begrime with filth.

It was the cuſtom with cheating beggars formerly, and, I believe, is not yet out of practice with them, to raiſe artificial ſores on their bodies to move compaſſion, by burning crow's-foot, ſpearwort, and ſalt, together, and, clapping them at once on the face, it fretted the ſkin; then, with a linen rag, which ſticks cloſe, they tear off the ſkin and ſtrew on a little powder of arſenic which gives it an ugly and ill-favoured

 look:

look: theſe ſores are, in the canting phraſe, called *clegms*.

IDEM.

Strike, in their numb'd and mortify'd bare arms,
Pins, wooden pricks, nails, &c.

Hypocriſy is of all nations and all ages. The practice of the religious cheats, in the Eaſt Indies, at this day, is to drive a piece of iron through ſome part of the body, which for ſome time gives great pain to the ſufferer: theſe raſcals on this account are held ſo ſacred that nobody dares offend them.

Scene IV.

LEAR.

Oh! how the mother ſwells upward to my heart.

So in Julius Cæſar, act IV. Caſſius to Brutus.

Have you not love enough to bear with me,
When that raſh humour, which my mother gave me,
Makes me forgetful?———

LEAR.

Do you but mark, how this becomes the houſe?
Dear daughter, I confeſs that I am old;

Age

Age is unneceſſary: on my knees I beg,
That you'll vouchſafe me raiment, bed, and food.

This preſents to the ſpectator a moſt ſtriking picture of an unhappy aged parent, who finds himſelf reduced to the neceſſity of repreſenting, in his own perſon, by action, the abſurdity, as well as wickedneſs, of his childrens conduct to him. This was a dramatic ſituation utterly unknown to Booth, Boheme, and Quin, becauſe this affecting paſſage was omitted in Tate's alteration of Lear. It was happily reſtored by Mr. Garrick, who knew its beauty. He threw himſelf on both knees, with his hands claſped, and, in a ſupplicating tone, repeated this touching, though ironical, petition.

IDEM.

Thy *tender-hefted* nature.

By *hefted* Mr. Steevens thinks the author means *heaved*; a boſom agitated by tender paſſions. I ſuppoſe the expreſſion was intended to ſignify *ſmooth*, or *ſoft-handled*, conſequently put here for *gentleneſs of diſpoſition.* *Heft* or *handled*; Teutonicè *haft*; Belgicè *heft.* *Minſhew's Dictionary.*

IDEM.

——— Her eyes are fierce, but thine
Do comfort, and not burn.

Maſſinger, who admired and imitated our author, had this paſſage in his eye in his Baſhful Lover.

———— Let your beams,
Warm and comfort, not conſume, me.

IDEM.

———— If your ſweet ſway
Allow obedience. ———

To Mr. Steevens's various quotations, in ſupport of the old reading *allow*, in oppoſition to Dr. Warburton's *hallow*, let us add the deciſive authority of Shakſpeare himſelf, in his Timon of Athens, act V. where the ſenator tells Alcibiades, that he ſhall be

Allow'd with abſolute power.

That is, *Inveſted with ſupreme authority.*

LEAR.

LEAR.

——— And, 'ſquire-like, penſion beg,
To keep baſe life on foot. ———

To beſtow a penſion on virtue and merit is conferring honour on the donor and receiver, but there ſurely cannot be a meaner character than the man, who, without any ſervice performed to his king and country, maintains himſelf by a gratuitous income.

IDEM.

——— Touch me with noble anger.

Dr. Warburton is continually making our old bard deeply verſed in antient learning, and particularly in the more abſtruſe parts of mythology. Shakſpear's meaning in this place is very obvious; let me, ſays Lear, finding himſelf give way to the weakneſs of humanity occaſioned by his daughters unexampled inſolence and cruelty, bear my misfortunes like a king and a man, by requiting diſobedience and ingratitude with wrath, resentment, and revenge, and not melt into tears, sighs, and womanish lamentations.

CHAPTER

CHAPTER XXXII.

Nuncle. — *Court holy-water.* — *Caitiff* — *Derived from the Italian.* — *Nero an angler in the infernal regions.* — *Wit borrowed from Lucian.* — *Tom Brown.* — *Deprivation of ſight, a Norman puniſhment.* — *William the Conqueror.* — *Polymneſtor and OEdipus.* — *Manner of putting out Gloſter's eyes.* — *Gold-beaters ſkin.* — *Gloſter by Quin* — *Berry* — *Davies.* — Our mean ſecures us. — *Lines of Dryden.* — Slaves heaven's ordinance *diſcuſſed.* — *Dover cliff.* — I fear your diſpoſition. — *Miſtake of Dr. Johnſon.* — Better day — *Farther explained.* — *The ſteward's fidelity.* —*The word* attached.—But to the girdle do the gods inherit. — *Brantome quoted.* — *Edgar generous.* — *Woman's will.* — *The moſt pathetic of all interviews.* — *Soul in bliſs.* — *Purgatory.* — *Greek tragedians.* — *Shakſpeare's characters ſuperior to all others.*

others. — *Garrick inimitable.* — *Mrs. Cibber's Cordelia.* — *Mrs. Davies.* — *Burbage and Taylor.* — *Wilks.* — *George Powell.* — *Smith.* — *Ryan.* — *Havard.* — *Reddiſh.* — *Shakſpeare a moraliſt.* — *Edmund's remorſe.* — *Tom Walker.* — *Paſſages explained.* — *Tate's additional ſcenes.* — *Garrick's look and action.* — Old Lear ſhall be a king again. — *Particular reſpect paid to the tragedy of Lear.* — *Garrick's maſterpiece.* — *Three characters.* — *Martyrs to virtue.* — *Story of a young actreſs.*

FOOL.

O *nuncle*, court holy-water, in a dry houſe, is better than the rain-water out of door.

N*UNCLE*, or *uncle*, was formerly a provincial term of regard from the loweſt of the people to their ſuperiors, and not yet obſolete in ſome parts of Shropſhire, &c. By court holy-water being better than rain-water, the Fool plainly wiſhes that Lear would return to his daughters; for flattery, he he inſinuates, is better in a warm houſe than plain dealing in the midſt of a ſtorm.

KENT.

——— Man's nature cannot carry
The affliction nor the fear.

It is not in humanity to endure the violence or the affright which attends ſuch a dreadful ſtorm.

LEAR.

Caitiff, ſhake to pieces.

The commentators derive the word *caitiff* from captive, or the French word *chetif*. It is perhaps deduced from the Italian word *cativo*, baſe, wicked, profligate. It is ſo underſtood by Berkley in his Ship of Fools:

That none wiſe or good will commit this offence;
For all are *Caytiffes* that are of this lewd ſort.

IDEM.

Poor fool and knave, I have one part in my heart
That's ſorry yet for thee.

Amidſt all his afflictions, Lear recollects that he has brought misfortune and ſufferance on thoſe who uſed to look up to him for protection and kindneſs. This is one of thoſe happy touches of Shakſpeare, where humanity

humanity triumphs over ſelfiſhneſs; and, it is to ſuch abundant moral and pathetic applications to our feelings, that he owes a great part of that preference we give him over all other dramatic writers.

Scene VI.

EDGAR.

Fraterreto calls me, and tells me, *Nero* is an angler in the lake of darkneſs.

This is borrowed from Rabelais; and it is an imitation of him who derived the idea of giving trades to emperors, kings, and other great men, in the infernal regions, from Lucian. In his Menippus ſeu Necyomantia, he introduces kings and grandees begging, ſelling ſalt-fiſh, and teaching elements of learning to ſupply their neceſſities.

Πολλω δ'αν οιμαι μαλλον εγελας, &c. — "You would have ſmiled to ſee ſome of our kings and ſatraps turned beggars there, or ſelling ſalt-fiſh for their bread, or teaching

teaching ſchool, ſcoffed at and buffeted like the meaneſt ſlaves. I could ſcarce contain myſelf when I ſaw Philip of Macedon there, as they pointed him out to me in a corner, healing the wounds of old ſhoes."

Franklin's Lucian, vol. I. 8vo.

This ſingle hint of the great original father of humour has produced innumerable imitations of the ſmaller wits. Tom Brown is perhaps one of the beſt as well as moſt fruitful in this kind of infernal drollery.

GLOSTER.

By the kind gods.

There is no occaſion for any oſtentation of learning or acuteneſs here. *Kind* is a general term for good, bounteous, merciful.

CORNWALL.

Upon theſe eyes of thine I'll ſet my foot.

In ſome of the old Engliſh plays, written by Marlow, Marſton, Ford, and others, we we find ſhocking inſtances of mutilated limbs, of pulling out eyes, &c. but nothing in all Shakſpeare reſembling this ſhocking act of Cornwall. This violence, committed againſt humanity by the deprivation of ſight, was, I think, peculiar to the Normans, and almoſt unknown to this iſland till the times of William the Conqueror. Our old hiſtorians relate many terrible barbarities committed by this unrelenting and victorious tyrant upon his unhappy Engliſh ſubjects; and, amongſt many other ſpecies of cruelty, the evulſion of the eyes was not unfrequent. We are told that the purity of the Grecian ſtage would not permit any tranſaction of this kind to be brought before the ſpectators. But the Polymneſtor, of Euripides, whoſe eyes are put out by Hecuba and her maids, is produced to the audience hideouſly lamenting his misfortune. The blind OEdipus, of Sophocles, in a pathetic addreſs to Creon and the Chorus, recommends his daughters to their care and protection.

No

No authority, of ancient or later date, will juſtify the exhibition of a ſpectacle which affrighted nature ſhrinks from. —— Some very high reward ought to be given to an audience who are obliged to view ſo diſguſting a ſight as a human creature when his eyes are torn from their ſockets; voluntarily or involuntarily, it matters not. The cruel and ſordid Polymneſtor might, indeed, as he deſerved, have been puniſhed with the loſs of ſight, and not have been brought on the ſtage afterwards; and diſmiſſed, like ſome of Shakſpeare's characters, when dying, with a prophecy in his mouth. The ſpeech of OEdipus, after he has pulled out his eyes, is really affecting, but not of ſuch excellence as to recompence the ſpectators for ſo mortifying a ſpectacle.

That the tragedy of Lear, as originally written, did not pleaſe the audience, when acted, ſoon after the Reſtoration, by Betterton and his company, I have proved, as far as probability will warrant me, by Downs: nor can it be ſurpriſing, that the ſpectators ſhould be ſhocked

ſhocked at ſo horrible a ſight as one man ſtamping upon the eyes of another, and at the ſame time encouraged to proceed in his barbarity by one of the ſofter ſex! After all, Shakſpeare might poſſibly contrive not to execute this horrible deed upon the ſtage, though it is ſo quoted in the book. He was extremely careful of offending the eyes, as well as ears, of the ſpectators, by any thing outrageous. Gloſter's loſing his eyes is ſo eſſential to the plot, that Mr. Colman found it impoſſible to throw it out. However, at the preſent, the ſufferer is forced into ſome adjoining room; and the ears of the audience are more hurt by his cries than their eyes can be when he is afterwards led on the ſtage. The goldbeaters ſkin, applied to the ſockets, as if to ſtaunch the bleeding, abates ſomething perhaps of the hideouſneſs of the ſpectacle.

I have already ſaid, that Quin was juſtly celebrated for his performance of Gloſter. He was ſucceeded by Hulet, a man of great merit in the ſock and buſkin. At Drury-lane,

lane, the elder Mills acted Glofter with Booth. Ned Berry, a man of very confiderable abilities in a great variety of parts, was Garrick's Glofter for many years. —— His countenance was expreffive, his figure large and important, his voice fonorous, and his feelings of paffion full and energetic. When ficknefs deprived the ftage of this valuable man, Mr. Garrick called upon the writer of this Mifcellany to reprefent the part of Glofter; the candour of the audience gave him much more encouragement than he expected.

Act IV.

GLOSTER.

———— Full oft 'tis feen,
Our *mean* fecures us, and our mere defects
Prove our commodities.

Dr. Warburton's *mediocre* and *moderate*, for *mean*, are approved by Mr. Steevens. I fhould wifh to go a little farther than *mediocrity* or *competency*. Shakfpeare intends, in my opinion, by this term, that fituation in life which is ſo low as to excite no envy from rivals or fear from ſuperiors. Inſignificancy of character and deficiency in means are often, I believe, according to the mind of Gloſter, real advantages.

If more were neceſſary to eſtabliſh this interpretation of the word *mean*, two lines, attributed to Dryden, in the altered Macbeth, and ſpoken by Macduff when he takes leave of his wife, will, I hope, be deemed not foreign to the purpoſe :

> You to your weakneſs all your ſafety owe,
> As graſs eſcapes the ſcythe by being low.

IDEM.

> Let the ſuperfluous and luſt-dieted man,
> Who *ſlaves heaven's ordinance*, &c.

There cannot, in my opinion, be a happier expreſſion than than that of *ſlaving the ordinance of heaven* ; though Dr. Warburton would ſubſtitute *brave* ; and Dr. Johnſon thinks, *to ſlave an ordinance* may ſignify *to ſlight or ridicule it*. But the contemptuous hypocrite makes the laws of heaven his property ; he puts them on for convenience, and throws them aſide for the ſame

purpoſe ;

purpoſe; they are his ſtalking horſe, to reach what he aims at; for this reaſon, they are, with great propriety, termed his *ſlaves*, whom he abuſes at will. Mr. Steevens rightly obſerves, that to *ſlave* an ordinance, is to treat it like a *ſlave*, and make it ſubject to us.

IDEM.

There is a cliff, whoſe high and bending head
Looks fearfully on the confined deep.

Southern had this paſſage, probably, in his eye, in the fifth act of Oroonoko:

—— Oh! for a whirlwind's wing,
To carry us to yonder cliff, that *frowns*
Upon the flood!

Scene II.

ALBANY, [TO GONERIL.]
I fear your diſpoſition.

When I reflect upon your monſtrous ingratitude and cruelty to your indulgent father, I fear leſt heaven ſhould diſpoſe of you in ſuch a manner as to make you a terrible example of its vengeance. There cannot be a better commentary, on this text, than the words which fell from one of Cornwall's

 ſervants,

ſervants, who had been an eye-witneſs of Regan's brutal behaviour to Gloſter:

——— If ſhe live long,
And in the end meet the old courſe of death,
Women will all turn monſters.

MESSENGER.

A ſervant that he bred, thrill'd with *remorſe* —

Remorſe, in Shakſpeare, generally ſignifies *pity*, not *compunction*.

GONERIL.

One way, I like this well.

Dr. Johnſon thinks Goneril is pleaſed that Cornwall is deſtroyed, who was preparing to make war on her and her huſband; but is afraid of loſing Edmund to the widow. But, on the contrary, Albany and Cornwall were both united, notwithſtanding ſome ſmall differences, called, by Kent, *ſnuffs and packings*, between them, againſt Lear, Cordelia, and their French allies. Goneril's liking might proceed

proceed from a ſuggeſtion, that it would be no difficult matter to wreſt her ſiſter's dominions from her now her huſband was removed. If Cornwall died without iſſue, Goneril was preſumptive heireſs to Regan.

Scene III.

GENTLEMAN.

——— You have ſeen
Sunſhine and rain at once. Her ſmiles and tears
Were like a *better day*.

The laſt editors of Shakſpeare have very judiciouſly abſtained from altering an old reading, where ſenſe could be made of it, for a better. Dr. Warburton propoſes, inſtead of *better day*, to ſubſtitute *a wetter May*, with much plauſibility. Mr. Steevens has well ſupported the text as it now ſtands. I beg leave to add, to what that gentleman has advanced, that *the ſmiles of a better day* is relatively juſt. For, as days, in the beginning of ſummer, with a mixture of rain and ſunſhine, are a pleaſing promiſe of the fruits of the earth to follow; ſo the tears and ſmiles of Cordelia were good omens of her reſolution to bring relief and aſſiſtance to her father.

Scene V. Regan and Oſwald.

Dr. Johnſon wonders that Shakſpeare ſhould repreſent the Steward, who is a mere agent of baſeneſs, capable of fidelity. When a man is amply rewarded, for his iniquitous compliances with the commands of his ſuperiors, it is but natural to imagine he will be true to his employers, eſpecially as he will have reaſon to dread the puniſhment which would be inflicted for his diſobedience. That ſuch a wretch ſhould be anxious, when dying, for the delivery of that letter which he would not ſuffer to be unſealed, is not very ſurpriſing; it was only the conſequence of his purſuing the track of his accuſtomed practice.

EDGAR.

EDGAR.

——— How fearful
And dizzy 'tis to caſt one's eyes ſo low! &c.

This is a view of Dover-cliff, taken by a man, who aſſumes affright, which he feels not, in order to raiſe it in another. In thoſe, who view it now, it does not raiſe any extraordinary terror; for, in all probability, the altitude is ſomething diminiſhed ſince the days of Shakſpeare. The aſcent to it is eaſy, and the proſpect from it nothing alarming.

IDEM.

Ten maſts *at each* make not the altitude.

Mr. Pope altered *at each*, to *attach'd*; and Dr. Johnſon thinks it may ſtand, if the word was known in our author's time. — Minſhew, who publiſhed his Dictionary of nine Languages in 1617, a year after Shakſpeare's death, explains the word in the ſenſe it is applied by Mr. Pope:

Attach, to tack or faſten together.

Scene VI. Lear, Glofter, Edgar.

The diftraction of Lear, in this progrefs of the play, is wrought up to the higheft pitch of frenzy. The author avails himfelf of the fituation, in which he has placed his principal character, to introduce, from his mouth, fome very fevere and pointed fatire: equal to any that can be read in any ancient or modern writer.

LEAR.

But to the girdle do the gods inherit.

Whether Shakfpeare had read Brantome, part of whofe works had, I believe, been publifhed before this tragedy was acted, I know not; but that free writer, in his Lives of his amorous old Dames, tells us of an agreeable converfation he once had, with a beautiful and worthy *(honefte)* lady, when he was at the court of Spain. Amongft other choice matter, fhe obferved to him, *Que ningunas damas lindas fe hacen viejas de la cinta hafta a baxo,* That no fine women

women were ever old from the girdle downwards.—— The reſt of Brantome's converſation with this good lady may poſſibly entertain the reader; and I ſhall give it in the Frenchman's own words, which, on account of their naïveté, are, I think, not eaſily tranſlated:

Sur quoy je luy demanday comment elle l'entendoit? ſi c'étoit de la beauté du corps, depuis cette ceinture juſques en bas, qu'elle n'en diminuaſt par la vieleſſe; ou pour l'envie et l'appetit de la concupiſcence, qui ne vinſſent à ne n'eſteindre ni à ſe refroidir aucunement par le bas? --- Elle repondit, qu'elle entendoit et pour l'une et pour l'autre: car, pour ce qui eſt de la picqueure de la chaire, diſoit-elle, ne faut pas penſer qu'on ſe guériſſe juſques à la mort, quoique l'uſage y veuille répugner.

LEAR.

Draw the curtains.

The author of Rabelais's Life puts theſe words into his mouth when dying; upon what authority I know not.

EDGAR.

EDGAR.

To know our enemies' minds we'd rip their hearts.

To put enemies to the rack, to extort confeſſion, is ſurely not the meaning of the generous Edgar, as Dr. Warburton ſuppoſes. The probable intention of the author is, 'If, to acquire the knowledge of our enemies' intentions againſt us, we put in practice every allowable act, it ſurely can be no breach of good manners to unſeal and read their letters!'

IDEM.

O undiſtinguiſh'd ſpace of woman's will!

Dr. Warburton indulges himſelf with ſome ſevere ſatire againſt the fair ſex, by an illiberal interpretation of this paſſage.— But he might have ſpared Virgil's *Varium et mutabile ſemper femina*, as well as Sancho's arch proverb. Edgar's reflection imports no more, than that a vicious woman ſets no bounds to her appetites: ſuch an an one he knew Goneril was, and to her it is applied.

Scene VII.

In the progreſs of Lear's diſtraction, he is brought, by the poet, into a delirium; and, as the recovery from this ſituation is one of the moſt powerful efforts of the great poet's genius, to ſtop and view a little this moſt pathetic of all interviews, between a delirious father and his affectionate daughter, will not ſurely be called an oſtentatious parade of words or a feeble effort at panegyric. That, which does ſo much honour to the Engliſh ſtage, cannot be paſſed over as the mere effuſion of a common mind. One great deſign of Shakſpeare, in the choice of this fable, was to hold forth to mankind the unhappy conſequences of yielding to the ſudden and impetuous impreſſions of anger.

To trace the poet in his moral proceſs.—We ſee him introduce a character, amiable

in

in many reſpects, brave, generous, frank, and benevolent; but, at the ſame time, wilful, raſh, violent, and headſtrong. One unhappy reſolution, owing to the fervour of his diſpoſition, precipitates himſelf and his deareſt friends into inextricable ruin: from the ſhort fury of anger he is provoked, by the cunning of the ſcene, into unlimited reſentment, furious indignation, and the moſt violent rage. Conſequent agony and diſtreſs lead him to the door of madneſs. Reaſon is at length dethroned, and a high paroxyſm of frenzy ſucceeds. Nature affords ſome relief by a deliquium. Repoſe and medicinal application gently reſtore reaſon to her proper ſeat. Here, then, the interview opens, between the unhappy Father, juſt returning into ſenſation, and the pious Daughter watching with impatience for a parent's returning intelligence. How affecting is Cordelia's ſupplication, when ſhe kiſſes her ſleeping father! ——

———— Reſtoration, hang
Thy med'cine on my lips; and let this kiſs

Repair

Repair those violent harms that my two sisters
Have in thy reverence made!

I am sorry this most beautiful incident was overlooked in the representation. —— When Lear awakes, Shakspeare, forgetting that Lear is a heathen, puts into his mouth the words of one in purgatory:

Thou art a soul in bliss; but I am bound
Upon a wheel of fire, that mine own tears
Do scald like molten lead.

On Cordelia's falling on her knees, and imploring his benediction, Lear kneels to his daughter, not knowing who she was or what he did.

The several breaks and interruptions, of imperfect reason and recovering sense, are superior to all commendation, and breathe the most affecting pathos:

—— I am mightily abus'd!
I should die with pity to see another thus! —
I fear I am not in my perfect mind.

At

At laſt he recollects his dear Cordelia:

——— Do not laugh at me:
For, as I am a man, I think that lady
To be my child, Cordelia!

The audience, which had been ſighing at the former part of the ſcene, could not ſuſtain this affecting climax, but broke out into loud lamentations.

Be your tears wet?

ſays Lear, putting his hand upon the cheeks of Cordelia; as if he had ſaid, Can you really feel grief for one who ſo cruelly treated you?

IDEM.

——— Yes, faith!

I appeal to all, who are converſant in ancient or modern dramatic poetry, whether this ſcene of domeſtic ſorrow be not ſuperior, in compoſition, to all they ever read! The Greek tragedians, who deal much in demi-gods, too often raiſe their heroes

heroes above humanity. The French either imitate their manner, or make their principal characters too national. Shakſpeare alone draws ſuch men as all nations and all ages will acknowledge to be of kin to them. Cibber and others juſtly lament, that the beauties of elocution and action ſhould die with their poſſeſſors, and cannot, by any art, be tranſmitted to poſterity. They, who have had the exquiſite pleaſure to ſee Mr. Garrick in King Lear, will moſt unfeignedly wiſh that his action and elocution could have been perpetuated. A Reynolds could have faithfully tranſcribed a look and an attitude; but, alas! this would have been but an imperfect repreſentation. The wonders of his voice and multiplied expreſſion could not have been preſerved!

In the preceding ſcenes of Lear, Garrick had diſplayed all the force of quick tranſition from one paſſion to another: he had, from the moſt violent rage, deſcended to ſedate calmneſs; had ſeized, with unutterable ſenſibility, the various impreſſions of terror,

terror, and faithfully repreſented all the turbid paſſions of the ſoul; he had purſued the progreſs of agonizing feelings to madneſs in its ſeveral ſtages. Yet, after he had done all this, he exhibited himſelf, in this fine ſcene, in ſuch a ſuperior taſte, as to make it more intereſting than any thing the audience had already enjoyed. But indeed the incident itſelf is very ſtriking. --- Every ſpectator feels for himſelf and common humanity, when he perceives man, while living, degraded to the deprivation of ſenſe and loſs of memory! Who does not rejoice, when the creative hand of the poet, in the great actor, reſtores him to the uſe of his faculties!

Mrs. Cibber, the moſt pathetic of all actreſſes, was the only Cordelia of excellence. The diſcovery of Lear, in priſon, ſleeping with his head on her lap, his hand cloſed in her's, whoſe expreſſive look ſpoke more than the moſt eloquent language, raiſed the moſt ſympathiſing emotions. --- Mrs. Davies, during Mrs. Cibber's illneſs, was

was invited to ſupply her place. She did not pretend to imitate that which was not to be attained by imitation, the action, voice, and manner, of Mrs. Cibber. Mrs. Davies's figure, look, and deportment, were eſteemed to be ſo correſpondent with the idea of this amiable character, that ſhe was diſmiſſed with no inconſiderable ſhare of approbation.

Act V. Scene II.

EDGAR.

Draw thy ſword.

I fear it is almoſt uſeleſs, at this diſtance of time, to enquire who played the part of Edgar originally. If I might be indulged a conjecture, upon a matter ſo uncertain, I ſhould fancy that the characters of Lear and Edgar were given, by the author, to Burbage and Taylor, and that the latter was the Edgar. Though this actor was the original Hamlet, it is generally admitted that Burbage was the firſt tragic player

 of

of the age. Taylor was the Iago to Burbage's and Swanſton's Othello. Wilks, for many years, moſt probably from about 1705 to 1729, (when Lear was diſcontinued on account of Booth's illneſs,) pleaſed the public with his animated repreſentation of Edgar. Till the appearance of Barry, no lover like Wilks, ſince Mountfort, had ſtepped upon the Engliſh ſtage. That he acquired poſſeſſion of the part muſt have been owing to the irregular conduct of George Powell, who had ſtronger pretenſions of voice, figure, action, and manner, by the confeſſion even of Cibber, who ſeems to have hated Powell. Smith, on the revival of Lear by Tate, repreſented Edgar; but, on his death, in 1695, it was given to Powell. Wilks excelled in the ſcenes of love and gallantry, nor was he deficient in the aſſumed madneſs, of Edgar. Ryan, I have reaſon to believe, from what I heard from Roberts, the comedian, copied Powell's manner, whom he had attended to when very young. Not

to

to place Ryan on the ſame bench with Wilks, for that would be unjuſt, in the comic ſcenes of Edgar he diſplayed conſiderable ſkill. In the challenge of Edmund, Wilks was highly ſpirited, with ſuperior elegance of deportment. Ryan's whole behaviour, in the fight and challenge, was manly and feeling. Havard, who acted Edgar many years, had ſeen theſe actors in the part, and formed a very pleaſing manner from both. Nor muſt we forget the merit of the unfortunate Reddiſh; who, in the opinion of the public, and the great manager, his employer, was acknowledged to have well underſtood and repreſented the character.

EDGAR.

The gods are juſt, and from our pleaſant vices
Make inſtruments to ſcourge us.

Of all dramatic authors, ancient and modern, Shakſpeare is the moſt moral. Dr. Johnſon, in his admirable preface to our author, is of opinion, that his frequent moralizing did not proceed from premeditated intention or deſign. I ſhould imagine, that it muſt have formed one part of his general plan in the writing of his dramas, otherwiſe he could not have ſo frequently adopted that mode of writing; any more than a clergyman could, by chance, perpetually preach on moral, and never on poſitive, duties.

EDMUND.

This ſpeech of your's hath mov'd me.

The obdurate and cruel Edmund feels no tenderneſs and remorſe, till rouſed by the relation of his father's death, pathetically deſcribed by Edgar. This is finely touched, as well as artfully contrived, by the author; for it introduces the notice of Lear and Cordelia, for whom the audience muſt have been in pain.

Walker, the original Macheath, acted Edmund with a vigour and ſpirit which were only below his perſonating the Baſtard Falconbridge, in King John, on account of the inferiority of one character to another. When he ſpoke the firſt ſoliloquy, "Thou,

" Thou, Nature, art my goddeſs ! &c." the audience juſtified the ſelecting him for the daring and intrepid part. Walker's action, which was taught him by Booth, was extremely eaſy and natural : his tread was manly, and his whole behaviour and deportment diſengaged and commanding. I cannot, with equal praiſe, ſpeak of any other Edmund in Lear.

Scene X. and laſt.

[Lear brings in the dead Cordelia in his arms.]

KENT.

Is this the promis'd end ?

" Do all my hopes of Lear's reſtoration end in his diſtraction and the death of Cordelia ?"

EDGAR.

Or image of that horror !

" Is it not rather a ſcene of the moſt unſpeakable horror ?"

ALBANY.

Fall and ceaſe.

Perhaps Albany means, " Lower your voice, and ceaſe all exclamation, leſt you interrupt the dying King." This is not unlike, in ſenſe, to the word *quietneſs* in Antony and Cleopatra: Charmion, on the Queen's fainting, whiſpers to Iras, *O quietneſs!*

Succeſſive audiences, by their perſevering approbation, have juſtified the happy ending of this tragedy, with the reſtoration of Lear and the marriage of Cordelia and Edgar.

Though Tate's alterations are, in many places, mean, and unworthy to be placed ſo near the compoſition of the beſt dramatic author, it muſt be confeſſed, that, in the conduct of ſome ſcenes, whether contrived by himſelf, or hinted to him by his friend Dryden, he is not unhappy. One ſituation of his is particularly affecting: where the ſcene opens, and diſcovers Lear with his head on Cordelia's lap, and the King, in his

his ſleep, attacking the forces of his enemies. The bringing that action forward to the audience, which is only related in the old play, of Lear's killing the two ſoldiers employed to murder him and Cordelia, is a circumſtance that gives pleaſure and exultation to the ſpectators. The half-breathing and panting of Garrick, with a look and action which confeſſed the infirmity of old age, greatly heightened the picture. To ſpeak in Shakſpeare's phraſe, this incident will be *locked in the memory* of thoſe who have the pleaſure to remember it. Barry, in this ſcene, was a lively copy of Garrick's manner, and had the ſuperior advantage of a more important figure. Who could poſſibly think of depriving an audience, almoſt exhauſted with the feelings of ſo many terrible ſcenes, of the inexpreſſible delight which they enjoyed, when the old King, in rapture, cried out ——

Old Lear ſhall be a king again!

In this laſt, and the foregoing, ſpeech of Lear, Booth was inimitably expreſſive,

 from

from the full tones of his voice and the admirable manner of harmonizing his words, Upon the whole, Booth rendered the character of Lear more amiable, or, to ſpeak critically, leſs terrible, than Garrick.— The latter went more deeply into his author's meaning; and expreſſed the various paſſions of the character with ſuch truth and energy, that no audience ever ſaw him without aſtoniſhment as well as rapture. There was a particular compliment paid to the exhibition of this tragedy, beyond all others. After a very loud plaudit at the end of the play, when the curtain was let fall, the ſpectators teſtified their complete pleaſure and ſatisfaction, by renewing their loud applauſes two or three ſeveral times. —— Lear was, in the opinion of a great number of the beſt judges, Mr. Garrick's maſterpiece. When this inimitable actor was buried, a perſon, it is ſaid, by deſire of Mrs. Garrick, threw the play of Hamlet into the grave with the corpſe. With equal, if not more, propriety, Lear might have alſo been depoſited there.

Amongſt a number of Shakſpeare's capital plays, it is not eaſy to determine in which the genius of the writer ſhone out with greateſt luſtre. However, I believe it will be confeſſed, that in none of his tragedies the paſſions have been extended with more genuine force, the incidents more numerous or more dramatically conducted, nor the moral more profitable, than in Lear. There are three characters, in this play, of which I ſcarcely know that there are any counterparts in any other, ancient or modern. They are, indeed, all martyrs to virtue and piety. Though too much cannot be ſaid of the generous offspring of our inimitable bard, Kent can no where be matched. Edgar and Cordelia follow next: ſuch an example as Cordelia, of filial piety, except perhaps in the Grecian ſtage,* is not to be found in dramatic poetry. Edgar is equal in merit to the lady.

I ſhall

* The Antigone of Sophocles, in the Œdipus Colonæus, is a moſt perfect character of filial piety.

I ſhall conclude my obſervations on this tragedy with a theatrical anecdote.

Amongſt the actreſſes who perſonated Cordelia, when Boheme acted Lear, there was a young woman whoſe name was Stone. Her hiſtory is ſo ſingular, that I think it merits a place in this Miſcellany.

Miſs Stone's genteel figure, agreeable countenance, and pleaſing voice, recommended her to the notice of Mr. Rich; who, about the year 1725, employed her to act in his theatre of Lincoln's-inn Fields. The unaffected and elegant manner ſhe diſplayed in a variety of parts, chiefly ſuch as attract our notice from youth, modeſty, and gentleneſs, pleaſed the public. Mr. C———, a young gentleman, heir to a large eſtate, fell paſſionately in love with her. —— As he could not obtain her conſent to his addreſſes, without the matrimonial bond, the warmth of his paſſion impelled him to marry her. The father no ſooner heard of of this indiſcreet and diſproportioned match than he commanded his ſon to return home to the family ſeat, which was not many miles diſtant from the metropolis. The ſon, through dread of his father's diſpleaſure, obeyed; and the new-married pair were parted, never to meet again.

The family, ſhocked at the unequal match, determined, at all events, to bring about a ſeparation. In order to carry on their deſign, they prevailed on the manager of the playhouſe, by intimidation or other means, never to ſuffer Mrs. C. to act upon his ſtage. The next ſtep was to prove the wife's incontinency; and, to this end, they addreſſed themſelves to a gay man of faſhion, who was baſe enough to engage in their conſpiracy. This man made his addreſſes to Mrs. C. with a view to debauch her. The poor unhappy young woman, being ſeparated from her huſband, by fraudulent and oppreſſive arts deprived of the means of gaining a maintenance from the theatre,

and

and ſurrounded with poverty, fell a prey to the inſidious attempts of a man who had held out to her the means of preſent relief. The gentleman had no ſooner accompliſhed his ends than he forſook her. She ſoon after periſhed in great affliction and diſtreſs. Whether the huſband be ſtill living I know not. The man of faſhion became afterwards an eminent writer; I hope he ſincerely repented the ſhameful part he acted in this iniquitous tranſaction.

Antony

Antony and Cleopatra.

CHAPTER XXXIII.

Ben Jonson's ridicule on Shakspeare's Antony and Cleopatra. — Dr. Johnson's opinion of that tragedy.—May's Cleopatra.— Dryden's All for Love.— Sir Charles Sedley.— Fulvia's character.— Epigram of Augustus. — Tears of an onion.—*Mr. Steevens mistaken.* — Arm-gaunt steed *explained. — Cleopatra's* sallad-days. — *Several other passages interpreted.— K. Charles* I. *and Mr. Hyde. — Antony's bounty.* — Quick comedians.— *The custom of ridiculing all characters on the Athenian stage.—Lord-mayor of London and Lord Burleigh. — Custom of boys acting women's parts. — Shakspeare's female characters.— Who was the first actress that appeared on the London stage. — French actresses.—Spanish theatre.—Baretti's account of it. — The pope suffers none but eunuchs to*

play

play in operas. — Countryman and aſpic. — Cleopatra's noble preparation for death. — Whether killed by poiſon or the aſpic.— Her character. — Dr. Johnſon's criticiſm examined. — Garrick and Mrs. Yates.— Dryden's All for Love. — Booth and Oldfield.— Mills.—Wilks.—Colley Cibber.—Mrs. Porter.

BEN JONSON, in his Silent Woman, has apparently, though obliquely, treated this tragedy as a play full of nothing but empty noiſe and fights by ſea, with drum, trumpet, and target; nor does Dr. Johnſon, I think, rank it amongſt thoſe of our author's dramas which are greatly eſteemed. Yet, of all the plays written on the ſubject of Antony and Cleopatra, this moſt intereſts the paſſions, and conſequently is moſt dramatic. It repreſents more of action, character, and manners, than May's Cleopatra or Dryden's All for Love. As to the Antony and Cleopatra of Sir Charles Sedley, it was

was lucky for the author, that he wrote ſome years after the Rehearſal had been acted; or, in all probability, he would have made no inconſiderable figure in that comic ſatire.

It is true that there are not, in Shakſpeare's Antony and Cleopatra, as in many of our author's pieces, many ſtriking and important ſcenes. According to his plan, of crouding the greateſt part of Antony's life, from the death of Fulvia till he killed himſelf in Alexandria, that would not have been poſſible.

The minutiæ of events deſcribed leſſen the grandeur of the whole. The ſeveral pictures are, in themſelves, however, complete, and give great variety and entertainment; though it was impoſſible they ſhould be, all of them, either finely coloured or highly finiſhed. There is, in this play, perhaps, more of that general character by which Pope diſtinguiſhes our author from other great writers: "The genius of Shakſpeare ſtrikes ere we are

aware,

aware, like an accidental fire from heaven." The two principal characters are as wild and irregular in the ſcene as they were in their lives.

Sir Charles Sedley could either have no veneration for Shakſpeare, or had great confidence in his own abilities. He has borrowed very little from him, and has ſpoiled what he took. Dryden, on the contrary, ſeems to have been, in many ſcenes of his All for Love, inſpired with the warm flame of the original. In endeavouring to imitate his maſter, he has excelled himſelf. Ventidius is a ſober Enobarbus. Antony, in the firſt act, is ſo great, that the poet wanted power to keep pace with himſelf, and falls off from his firſt ſetting out. Dryden's Cleopatra has none of the various feminine artifices, and ſhapes of paſſions, of the original; nor, indeed, that greatneſs of ſoul which ennobles her laſt ſcenes in Shakſpeare. She reſembles more the artful kept-miſtreſs, than the

the irregular, but accomplished, Queen of Egypt.

Act I. Scene I.

CLEOPATRA.

When shrill-tongu'd Fulvia scolds.

Fulvia, successively the wife of Clodius, Curio, and Mark Antony, was a most extraordinary woman. She scorned all domestic employment; not content with governing her husbands at home, she aspired to rule over them in public, in the cabinet and the field, to direct their counsels, and to command their troops. She had, for a long time, an absolute power over Antony; whom she tamed so thoroughly, by the vigour of her spirit, that she left no work of that sort for Cleopatra. Cicero, in one of his Philippics, intimates, that he conceived great hopes of Antony's ruin from his connection with that turbulent woman. Rome, said the orator, had already received two payments from her, meaning the deaths of Clodius and Curio; and was in expectation of a third, by the speedy destruction of Antony. To this severe sarcasm we may perhaps attribute the shocking behaviour of this virago to the head of Cicero, when brought to her. With bitter upbraidings she placed it in her lap; she first extracted the tongue from the head; and afterwards, with the bodkin, pricked it several times, still uttering the most poignant and abusive expressions.† It is generally said, that her jealousy of Cleopatra excited her to make war upon Octavius. However, if we may believe the epigram, in Martial, attributed to Augustus, he might, if he pleased, have accommodated the matter upon easier terms than fighting. The spirit of this piece of wit consists in Fulvia's offering Octavius a share in her bed, or else threatening a struggle for conquest in the field. 'If that be the case,' the triumvir cried, 'sound trumpets

† Dion Cassius.

trumpets and beat drums, for any thing is preferable to this lady's favours.' This high-ſpirited dame was at laſt conquered by her huſband's neglect and reproaches. He ſeverely chid her, by letter, for raiſing diſturbances in Italy. She died at Sicyon, on the road to Athens; and this event accelerated a match between the amiable Octavia and Mark Antony.

Scene II.

CHARMION.

Nay, if an oily palm be not a fruitful prognoſtication, I cannot ſcratch my ear.

This is ſimilar to a paſſage in Othello, act III. where Othello, jealous of his wife, takes her by the hand:

This hand of your's is moiſt, my lady.

———— ————

There is a young and ſweating devil here,
That commonly rebels.

ENOBARBUS.

And, indeed, the tears live in an onion that ſhould water this ſorrow.

That is, ‘ Fulvia's death will cauſe no real grief in you; the tears, which you will ſhed on this occaſion, reſemble ſuch as are extracted by the application of an onion to the eye.’ *If you cannot cry, clap an onion to your eye*, has been, I believe, an old ſarcaſm on forced ſorrow. Suidas records a Greek proverb, which proves the power of an onion to draw tears: Κρομμυα εσθιειν, *Cepas edere:* and he quotes, from a loſt comedy of Ariſtophanes, Κρομμυα τ᾽αρ᾽ ȣκ εδη, αντι, ȣκ εκλαιε, *Cepas non comedit*, for *non flevit.*— Mr. Steevens has not, I think, underſtood the paſſage: an onion has, certainly, in contradiction to what he aſſerts, much moiſture in it.

CLEOPATRA.

Though you in ſwearing ſhake the throned gods.

So, in Timon, *And to ſtrong ſhudders ſwear th'immortal gods.*

ANTONY.

ANTONY.

——— But my full heart
Remains in uſe to you.

'I leave my heart with you as a pledge that I will never forſake you.'

Scene V. Cleopatra, Iras, &c.

ALEXAS.

And ſoberly did mount an *arm-gaunt ſteed.*

Much has been ſaid about the meaning of *arm-gaunt ſteed.* In ridicule, I ſuppoſe, of Warburton's explanation, Mr. Edwards compared the horſe, that bore the great maſter of a third part of the globe, to the lean and emaciated Roſinante of Don Quixote. Dr Johnſon would ſuppoſe him to be a poſt-horſe; as if Antony were reduced to the neceſſity of taking up with ſuch horſes as were to be found at an inn upon the road. I think the Emperor might, at leaſt, be allowed the ſame liberty which Jack Falſtaff aſſumed, when he heard his old friend and companion, Prince Hal, was king: *The laws of England are at my command; let us take any man's horſes!* We may reaſonably ſuppoſe, that the horſe, which bore Mark Antony, was remarkable for ſize and beauty. The Romans were particularly attentive to the breed, as well as management, of horſes. *Arm-gaunt* means *fine-ſhaped*, or *thin-ſhouldered. I muſt ſuppoſe*, ſays Bracken, *that every one is ſenſible that thin-ſhouldered horſes move the beſt.*—*Arm-gaunt*, I think, is a word compounded of the Latin word, *armus*, and *gaunt*; the latter is an old word well known; and *armus*, a ſhoulder, originally ſignified that part of a man's body, but the Latin writers afterwards more frequently applied it to the animal.

CLEOPATRA.

———— My *ſallad-days*,
When I was green in judgement, cold in blood.

The Queen talks like a woman well experienced in love-matters. Her commerce with

with Cæſar commenced when ſhe was young, and he was advanced to the fifty-fourth year of his age. Mark Antony was in the warm ſummer of life when he firſt beheld this wonder of attraction, having not ſeen more than thirty-three or thirty-four years. In comparing her two lovers, Cleopatra may well be juſtified in calling her firſt paſſion, 'the effects of her *ſallad-days*, greenneſs of judgement and coldneſs of blood."

Scene IV.

LEPIDUS.

His faults in him ſeem as the ſpots of heav'n,
More fiery by night's blackneſs.

Exactneſs of expreſſion muſt not be expected from a writer who takes up with the firſt words that come in his way. It is very plain, that Shakſpeare, by the night's blackneſs, meant only the abſence of the ſun. The ſtars ſhine brighteſt when the blaze of day is abſent.

OCTAVIUS.

——— Say this becomes him,
(As his compoſition muſt be rare indeed,
Whom theſe things cannot blemiſh.)

I cannot think, with Dr. Johnſon, that Cæſar's argument is inconſequent. It is a very common mode of expreſſion to ſay, that "ſuch a perſon is guilty of many abſurdities, which his friends will ſay, perhaps, become him; and ſuppoſe I ſhould grant all this, though he muſt be a very extraordinary man indeed if they do, yet, &c." The parentheſis does not hurt the logical concluſion of the main propoſition. Dr. Johnſon's reading is a very good explanation of the text.

Scene V.

CLEOPATRA.

——— And great Pompey
Would ſtand, and make his eyes grow in my brow;
There would he anchor his aſpect, and die
With looking on his life.

This

This is finely imitated, by Southern, in a beautiful apoſtrophe to Imoinda by the tender and paſſionate Oroonoko :

My ſoul ſteals from my body through my eyes;
All that is left of life I'll *gaze away*,
And die upon the pleaſure!

The image is alſo copied by the learned and elegant Fenton, in his Mariamne, though not ſo warmly, yet in conformity to the object and occaſion.

Mariamne, taking leave of her beloved infant, juſt going to be made a hoſtage at Rome, among other tender ſentiments, breaks out into the following:

No more muſt theſe deſiring eyes be fix'd
In ſilent joy with gazing on thy charms!

Act II. Scene II.

Octavius, Antony, Lepidus, &c.

CÆSAR.

Sit.

ANTONY.

Sit, ſir.

CÆSAR.

CÆSAR.

Nay, then.

Mr. Steevens is of opinion, that Antony is offended at the aſſumed ſuperiority of Cæſar, in bidding him ſit who was his equal. Can we ſuppoſe that Antony would come from Egypt to renew his friendſhip with Octavius, and take umbrage at a mere matter of form? Nothing paſſes between the triumvirs but what every body would expect. One politely invites the other to take his ſeat. The other returns the civility. Octavius puts an end to the ceremony, by ſaying, *Nay, then:* that is, 'Let us not protract time by needleſs form.' Antony, during the whole ſcene, is modeſt and temperate; and is rather the apologiſt than vindicator of his paſt conduct.

ENOBARBUS.

——— Your conſiderate ſtone.

Αγελαστος πετρα, *the unlaughing ſtone*, is an old Greek proverb; and *As dumb or dead*

as

as a ſtone is familiar, I ſhould think, to moſt languages. Mr. Steevens's conceit of the marble ſtatue is more ingenious than ſolid.

ANTONY.

I did not think to draw my ſword 'gainſt Pompey;
For he hath laid ſtrange courteſies and great
Of late upon me. I muſt thank him only
Leſt my remembrance ſuffer ill report:
At heel of that, defy him.

Dr. Johnſon ſays, on this paſſage, that Antony, unwilling to be thought forgetful of benefits, ſays, ' I muſt barely return him thanks, and then defy him.' This cannot, I think, be Shakſpeare's intention. One man receives great and unexpected favours from another. How does he repay them? by barely returning thanks to the kind donor, and then hurling defiance in his teeth! More is ſurely underſtood: ' Let me firſt,' ſays Antony, ' return the obligation I owe Pompey in ſuch a manner as becomes me; and then I ſhall think

think myſelf at liberty to join with you in declaring war againſt him.'

Scene II.

CLEOPATRA.

O that his fault ſhould make a knave of thee,
That art not what thou art ſure of!

Theſe lines have much perplexed the commentators. But a ſmall alteration in the pointing, and the addition of a ſingle letter, will remove all difficulties.

Cleopatra cannot endure to hear of Antony's marriage; and, notwithſtanding the Meſſenger perſeveres in telling her the ſame ſtory, ſhe perſiſts in aſking repeatedly whether he is married or not: at laſt, as if ſhe had been ſated with diſagreeable confirmations of what ſhe wiſhed not to believe, ſhe laments that Antony's crime ſhould make the Meſſenger diſhoneſt, who in reality was not ſo. But, the odious marriage ſtill haunting her memory, before ſhe diſmiſſes him ſhe adds, 'What! thou art ſure of it!' that is, 'He is certainly

tainly married!' The Meſſenger, we may ſuppoſe, confirms by action what he had ſo often affirmed in words; and ſhe then diſmiſſes him. The lines, then, with this trifling alteration, will read thus:

O that his fault ſhould make a knave of thee,
That art nôt!—What! thou'rt ſure of't!—Get thee
hence!

Scene III.

CÆSAR.

Will this ſatisfy him?

ANTONY.

With the health that Pompey gives him, elſe he is a very epicure.

Antony's anſwer is ironical: 'Lepidus, with the help of wine, will take up with this ſolution of his queſtion: but, when he is ſober, his judgement is ſo ſtrong, that he is a perfect epicure in the art of doubting.'

ENOBARBUS.

ENOBARBUS,

[ON SEEING LEPIDUS CARRIED OFF DRUNK.]

There's a ſtrong fellow, Menas.

MENAS.

——— Why?

ENOBARBUS.

——— He bears
The third part of the world, man; ſeeſt not?

MENAS.

The third part, then, is drunk.

As Lord Cheſterfield was going from the rooms at Bath to his apartments, he ſaw ſomebody carried home drunk in a chair. He aſked who it was? 'Quin, my lord, going home from the Three Tuns.' ——— 'That is a miſtake, ſir,' replied his lordſhip, 'for he has carried one of the three tuns home in his belly.'

Act

Act III. Scene V.

CLEOPATRA.

What ſhall we do, Enobarbus?

ENOBARBUS.

—— *Think and die.*

Hanmer has propoſed *Drink and die,* and brings Plutarch's ſtory of a ſocial club to ſupport his reading. Had Enobarbus been aſked this queſtion at a feaſt, or a drinking-bout, the anſwer would have been in character: but, to a ſerious queſtion, propoſed to an eminent ſoldier by a queen, ſuch a reply would have been improper, and indeed brutal, nor would his character of humour have excuſed it. Beſides, his anſwer to the next queſtion, put to him by Cleopatra, 'Whether ſhe or Antony was in fault?' without any farther examination, confirms the reading as preſerved by the laſt editors.

ENOBARBUS.

ENOBARBUS.

——— And be ſtaged to the ſhow
Againſt a ſworder.

'——— Fight with him, like a gladiator upon a ſtage, for the diverſion of the populace.'

ANTONY.

But, when we in our viciouſneſs grow hard,
O mis'ry on't! the wiſe gods ſeal our eyes.

This alludes to that doctrine which tells us,—when we become irreclaimable in our vices, heaven judicially blinds us.

IDEM.

——— Nay, you were a fragment
Of Cneius Pompey's.

Not Pompey the Great, as Mr. Tollet imagines, but his eldeſt ſon, Cneius.

IDEM.

Let a fellow that will take rewards.

That is, 'Suffer a poor menial ſervant to be familiar with you, whoſe condition in in life ſubjects him to the meanneſs of taking vails, or ſmall preſents, for officious attendance.'

IDEM.

Would you flatter one who *ties his points?*

Tying of points, in our author's time, was the office of a menial ſervant, or, as we now ſay, a valet de chambre: hence, metaphorically, it ſignifies a low and ſervile office. When Mr. Hyde, afterwards Earl of Clarendon, ſome time before the beginning of the civil wars, waited upon Charles I. at Hampton-court, the king ſaid to him, 'So, Ned Hyde, *they ſay you tie my points!*'

IDEM.

——— When my hours
Were *nice* and lucky.

The word *nice* has many ſignifications in Shakſpeare and other old Engliſh writers. Here Antony certainly means, 'When my time was ſpent in pleaſure, gaiety, and happineſs.'

IDEM.

Let's mock the midnight bell.

The pleaſures of revelling all night, and extending them to the morning, are often mentioned with glee by our author; but no where more pleaſantly than when noted by Falſtaff, who calls a midnight debauch *the ſweet morſel of the night*.

IDEM.

——— The next time I do fight,
I will make death love me; for I will contend
Ev'n with his peſtilent ſcythe.

Something very like the two firſt half-lines we find in Meaſure for Meaſure, ſpoken by Claudio to Iſabella:

——— If I muſt die,
I will encounter darkneſs as a bride,
And hug it in my arms.

Dryden, in his All for Love, act I. has nobly extended the whole paſſage, and more eſpecially the latter part of the quotation:

——— I

——— I long
Once more to meet our foes; that thou and I,
Like time and death, marching before our troops,
May taſte fate to them; mow them out a paſſage;
And, ent'ring where the foremoſt ſquadrons yield,
Begin the noble *harveſt* of the field.

Act IV. Scene II.

ANTONY.

——— Oh! my fortunes have
Corrupted honeſt men!

Admidſt all the folly, profligacy, and mad flights, of Mark Antony, ſome bright beams of a great and generous ſoul break forth with inimitable luſtre. Inſtead of reproaching his officer for deſertion and treachery, he lays the blame on his own adverſe fortune, which had unhappily overthrown the principles of the beſt and worthieſt men. This is one of our author's characteriſtical ſtrokes, and perfectly ſuited to Mark Antony.

SOLDIER,

[AFTER DELIVERING TO ENOBARBUS HIS TREASURE.]

——— Your emperor
Continues ſtill a Jove.

The bounty of Antony went hand in hand with his rapacity. As he omitted no means, however unjuſt, to acquire wealth, ſo he was equally liberal in beſtowing it. A lively ſentiment, or a ſmart repartee, would ſometimes recal him from the commiſſion of flagrant acts of injuſtice, though nothing could ſtop the floodgates of his generoſity. When he had reſolved to exact double taxes from the greateſt part of Aſia, he was told, if he perſiſted in his determination, he muſt alſo give that part of the world double ſeaſons, two winters and two ſummers in the year. This pertinent reproof prevented him from committing a cruel act of oppreſſion. To a perſon, whom he much befriended, he ordered his ſteward to give a very large ſum of money. The man thought the gift ſo exorbitant, that, to excite his cau-

tion

tion and convince him of his prodigality, he ſpread the money, in large heaps, upon ſeveral tables. The emperor, underſtanding the intention of the ſteward, and ſcorning to retract his order, ſaid, very coolly, 'that he thought the ſum of money had been much greater;' and commanded him to give his friend double the quantity.

SOLDIER.

We will purſue them into *bench holes.*

'We will purſue them, with blows, till we force them to ſeek for ſhelter under tables and *benches.*'

ANTONY.

Would'ſt thou be *window'd* in great Rome?

'Would'ſt thou be gazed at from *windows* and tops of houſes in the ſtreets of Rome?'

IDEM.

Pleach'd arms.

Arms tied behind him, as captives were obliged to walk after the victor's triumphal chariot.

EROS, [KILLING HIMSELF.]

— There, then! thus do I eſcape the ſorrow
Of Antony's death!

Eros generouſly killing himſelf, rather than be the inſtrument to murder his Emperor, is copied, with great judgement, by Dryden, in his All for Love, who has made a proper diſtinction between an old brother-officer and a freedman. Eros modeſtly begs from his maſter a parting farewel: Ventidius claims a laſt embrace, as from a friend. The paſſage deſerves to be quoted:

VENTIDIUS.

——— Give me your hand;
We ſoon ſhall meet again. Now farewel, emperor!
Methinks that word's too cold to be my laſt,
Since death ſweeps all diſtinction: farewel, friend!

Act. V. Scene I.

CÆSAR.

——— He *mocks*
The pauſes which he makes,

By

'By theſe wretched delays, he does but expoſe his conduct to deriſion.' *Mock* is a favourite word with Shakſpeare, and applied by him variouſly, but generally to vain and impotent endeavours.

IDEM.

——— Hear me, good friends.—
But I will tell you at ſome meeter ſeaſon.

So, in Julius Cæſar, Brutus, lamenting over the dead body of Caſſius,—

Caſſius, I ſhall find time, I ſhall find time!

Scene II.

PROCULEIUS.

——— You ſhall find
A conqueror that will pray in aid for kindneſs.

That is, 'he will himſelf turn ſolicitor for you.'

IDEM,

[AFTER PREVENTING CLEOPATRA FROM STABBING HERSELF.]

——— Hold, worthy lady, hold;
Do not yourſelf ſuch wrong, who are in this
Reliev'd, but not betray'd.

There is no neceſſity to alter the word *relieved* for *bereaved*, or any other word. *Relieved* alludes to a town beſieged, which, by the ſudden arrival of ſocial forces, is freed from the beſiegers.

CLEOPATRA.

This is the *brief* of money, &c.

'This is the *inventory*.'

IDEM.

Parcel the ſum of my diſgrace.

That is, adding another item to the groſs ſum of her misfortunes, by her ſteward's ingratitude.

IDEM.

IDEM.

——— The quick comedians
Extemporally will ſtage us.

Whether the comedians of Rome laid hold of every public matter, and turned it into a ſubject for ſtage-exhibition, is not, I believe, very certain. That the Engliſh comedians often bring on the ſtage, for their emolument, public, and ſometimes private, tranſactions, cannot be controverted. Let the Receipt-tax, a farce, be an inſtance. But, in ſuch matters, the Athenians excelled all mankind; for they, without diſtinction, brought upon their theatre all facts, faults, and blemiſhes, whatſoever. The old comedy exhibited, in perſon, the beſt as well as the worſt of the Athenian citizens, juſt as the malignity or humour of the author prompted. In their inferior dramatic pieces, the ſmalleſt defects of their demagogues, or public orators, were imitated and ridiculed. Any diſtinguiſhed pleaſantry of any man of note was ſure to be laid hold of by the Athenian

Athenian players, and expoſed to public view. Nor is there a more common expreſſion, in ſome of the old Greek critics, particularly the ſcholiaſt of Ariſtophanes, than that ſuch an one was brought upon the ſtage for ſome peculiarity or other in his gait, dreſs, look, manner of living; for his pride, extravagance, luxury, &c.

Something of this all ſtages have had in their original ſtate. When ſome great lords complained, to Louis XII. of France, that the comedians made free with his majeſty and the court, 'I am glad of it,' ſaid that good prince, 'for I ſhall be ſure to hear the truth;' and immediately gave orders that the comedians ſhould play before him, and deſired them to ſpare nobody. But this worthy king's good-nature is no excuſe for the licentiouſneſs of his players.—'The ſtage,' ſays honeſt Dodſley, in his preface to his edition of old Engliſh plays, 'no ſooner learned to ſpeak, than it grew ſcurrilous, and a chief magiſtrate of London complained, that Lord Burleigh had encouraged

encouraged the common players to represent his father on their ſtage.'

CLEOPATRA.

———— And I ſhall ſee
Some ſqueaking Cleopatra *boy* my greatneſs.

This refers to the cuſtom, in Shakſpeare's time, of boys, or young and handſome lads, acting women's parts. Our author ſometimes takes notice of the diminutive ſize of theſe boy-ladies. In Twelfth Night, Sir Toby Belch calls his niece's woman, 'the youngeſt of nine wrens.'— Some critics have ſuppoſed, that the female characters of Shakſpeare are not drawn with equal force and ſpirit, nor with that elegance and delicacy, as in other writers, on account of having ſuch improper repreſentatives. But I believe it will be difficult to find, in any author, ſuch abundant and varied orginality, in women's characters, as in Shakſpeare.* The ladies, indeed,

* Cleopatra, Juliet, Imogen, Ophelia, Lady Conſtance, Iſabella, Volumnia, Lady Macbeth, Portia in the

indeed, of Beaumont and Fletcher, are, in general, of a different complexion; few of them are marked with ſimplicity, elegance, modeſty, and ſenſibility; for the moſt part they are of the virago kind, bold, licentious, and violent, fitted for the tom-boys who acted them. Aſpaſia in the Maid's Tragedy, Juliana in the Double Marriage, Lucina in Valentinian, and a few more, are ſweet exceptions. —— Charles II. put an end to the ridiculous and abſurd cuſtom of men acting women's parts. A number of beautiful actreſſes ſoon gave a new luſtre to the Engliſh theatre. The firſt woman-actreſs was the grandmother of Norris, commonly called Jubilee Dicky. —— The French ſtage was, I believe, ſooner enlivened with women than the Engliſh, though they could boaſt of nothing but poor imitations of the ancients, till the days of Rotrou and Corneille. Baretti, in his Letters from Spain, acquaints us, that, till within theſe twen-

ty

the Merchant of Venice, Roſalind, Beatrice, are all diſtinct characters. To theſe many others might be added.

ty years, all the parts in Spaniſh plays were acted by women.* The pope permits none but men or eunuchs to play in the operas at Rome during the carnival.

CLOWN.

I know that a woman is a diſh for the gods, if the devil dreſs her not.

Shakſpeare well knew the taſte of a London audience. The ſeverity of the tragic ſcenes always wanted ſome comic relief; he has therefore brought in aid his conſtant friend, the joker, in the ſhape of a ſimple countryman.

CLEOPATRA.

——— Methinks I hear
Antony call; I ſee him rouſe himſelf,
To praiſe my noble act!

Cleopatra's preparation for death is animated to a degree of ſublimity which greatly raiſes the character of the Egyptian princeſs, and makes us lament her in death whom living we could not praiſe, though

* Vide the next chapter.

though it was impoſſible not to admire her.

It has been queſtioned, by ſome hiſtorians, whether Cleopatra was killed by drinking poiſon, which ſhe always carried about with her, or by the bite of the aſpic. Auguſtus confirms the latter account, by having her figure drawn with an aſpic on her arm, and expoſed to public view, when he triumphed over Antony.

* The beauty of Cleopatra was not very aſtoniſhing; ſhe did not, in feature, ſurpaſs many of her ſex: but the power of her wit greatly elevated her charms; her manner, too, was enchanting and irreſiſtible. No female could boaſt of ſuch a voice; for, ſo great was its variety of modulation, that it reſembled an inſtrument of many ſtrings. She is ſaid to have ſpoken above thirty languages; there were few foreign ambaſſadors to whom ſhe could not give audience in their own tongue.

I

* Plutarch.

I cannot help thinking that Dr. Johnſon has been rather precipitate in deciding upon the merit of Antony and Cleopatra. — How can I ſubmit to that ſentence, which pronounces, that there is no diſcrimination of character, in this play, except in Cleopatra, whom he conſiders only as conſpicuous for feminine arts? Thoſe ſhe has in abundance, it is true; but her generous reſolution, to die rather than ſubmit to embrace life upon ignoble terms, is ſurely alſo worth remembering. But is not Antony highly diſcriminated by variety of paſſion, by boundleſs generoſity, as well as unexampled dotage? What does this truly great writer think of Enobarbus, the rough old warrior, ſhrewd in his remarks and humorous in his plain-dealing? I ſhall ſay nothing of Octavius or Lepidus, though they are certainly ſeparated from other parts. The ſimplicity of the fable is neceſſarily deſtroyed, by exhibiting ſuch a croud of events, happening in diſtant periods of time, a fault common to hiſto-

rical

rical plays. But, in ſpite of all irregularities, this tragedy remains unequalled by any that have been written on the ſame ſubject.

Antony and Cleopatra had long lain dormant, I believe ever ſince it was firſt exhibited, when, about the year 1760, Mr. Garrick, from his paſſionate deſire to give the public as much of their admired poet as poſſible, revived it, as altered by Mr. Capel, with all the advantages of new ſcenes, habits, and other decorations proper to the play. However, it did not anſwer his own and the public expectation. It muſt be confeſſed, that, in Antony, he wanted one neceſſary accompliſhment: his perſon was not ſufficiently important and commanding to repreſent the part. There is more dignity of action than variety of paſſion in the character, though it is not deficient in the latter. The actor, who is obliged continually to traverſe the ſtage, ſhould from perſon attract reſpect, as well as from the power of ſpeech. Mrs. Yates

was

was then a young actress, and had not manifested such proofs of genius, and such admirable elocution, as she has since displayed; but her fine figure and pleasing manner of speaking were well adapted to the enchanting Cleopatra. Mossop wanted the essential part of Enobarbus, humour.

In Dryden's All for Love, Booth's dignified action and forcible elocution, in the part of Antony, attracted the public to that heavy, though, in many parts, well-written, play, six nights successively, without the assistance of pantomime or farce, which, at that time, was esteemed something extraordinary. But indeed he was well supported by an Oldfield, in his Cleopatra, who, to a most harmonious and powerful voice, and fine person, added grace and elegance of gesture. When Booth and Oldfield met in the second act, their dignity of deportment commanded the applause and approbation of the most judicious critics. When Antony said to Cleopatra,

You promis'd me your ſilence, and you break it
Ere I have ſcarce begun,

this check was ſo well underſtood by Oldfield, and anſwered with ſuch propriety of behaviour, that, in Shakſpeare's phraſe, *Her bendings were adornings.*

The elder Mills acted Ventidius with the true ſpirit of a rough and generous old ſoldier. To render the play as acceptable to the public as poſſible, Wilks took the trifling part of Dolabella, nor did Colley Cibber diſdain to appear in Alexas: theſe parts would ſcarcely be accepted now by third-rate actors. Still to add more weight to the performance, Octavia was a ſhort character of a ſcene or two, in which Mrs. Porter drew not only reſpect, but the more affecting approbation of tears, from the audience. Since that time, All for Love has gradually ſunk into fortgetfulneſs.

Rule

Rule a Wife and have a Wife.

CHAPTER XXXIV.

Plots of Beaumont and Fletcher taken from Spanish novels, and probably from Spanish plays. — Plot of Rule a Wife and have a Wife. — Character of an epicure, from Paulus Jovius. — Number of plays by Lope de la Vega. — Cervantes's account of the Spanish theatre.—Spanish Roscius, Lope de Rueda, his merit as an actor and writer.— Successor of Rueda.— Plays of Cervantes. — An opposer of Lope de la Vega.— A description of De Vega's uncommon genius.—Calderone, his successor; — debauches the public taste.— Remarkable passages in the life of De Vega.— His marriage and duel.— Secretary to Alva.—Soldier on-board the Spanish armada. — Second marriage. — His misfortunes. — Ordained priest.— Honoured with a degree by Pope Urban. — His death

 and

and magnificent funeral. — Gazed at when walking the ſtreets. — His great riches. — Works. — Quickneſs in compoſition. — His reaſons for breaking through the rules of the drama.—His extenſive benevolence and charity. — Chances and Rule a Wife, &c. — Garrick invited by Mr. Colman to revive plays of Beaumont and Fletcher and Maſſinger.— Revival of Philaſter and Bonduca.— Powell and Mrs. Yates. — Mr. Colman's edition of Beaumont and Fletcher. — Comedians obliged to Mr. Colman. — How. — Æſchylus, Sophocles, Plautus, Terence, Shakſpeare, and Moliere. — Firſt play of Shakſpeare.—His ſtyle imitated by Beaumont and Fletcher.— Their compoſition deſcribed. — Reaſon why the dialogue of Beaumont and Fletcher is generally more poliſhed than Shakſpeare's. — Mercutio. — Benedick. — Roſalind.— Prince of Wales and Falſtaff.— Licentious ſtyle of Beaumont and Fletcher. —Shakſpeare, compared to them, modeſt.— The Captain. — Scornful Lady and Cuſtom of the Country.—Shakſpeare's power over his auditors.

auditors. — Merchant of Venice. — Charles Macklin.—Wife for a Month.—Its plot and manners described at large. — Valerio and Evanthe.—Marriage Bed.— Lelia and her Father.— Real excellences of Beaumont and Fletcher flourish for ever.— Shakspeare one of the audience.— Dramatic effect.—Faithful Shepherdess. — Two noble Kinsmen. — Beaumont and Fletcher enviers of Shakspeare. — Rule a Wife and have a Wife acted by Hart and Mohun, &c. — The merit of the play. — Perez, a military coxcomb. — Cacafogo, a bastard Falstaff. — Elder Mills, Wilks, Booth, Mrs. Oldfield. — Ryan, Mrs. Younger. — Mossop desires to act Leon. — Opposed by Garrick. — Woodward.—Mrs. Cibber, in comedy, misplaced. — Mrs. Clive, Mrs. Pritchard, Mrs. Abington, and Mr. King. — Garrick's great skill in Leon. — The word feeling *explained.*

SEVERAL plots of Beaumont and Fletcher's plays are taken from Spanish novels, and, in all probability, from Spanish plays. To the first we owe the Chances, Love's Pilgrimage, and Rule a Wife and have a Wife, which are all taken from Cervantes. The last is formed entirely from the *Casamiento enganioso* of this celebrated writer. I am not sufficiently read in the theatre of Spain to point out the originals whence our authors might have borrowed fables, scenes, or characters. As they were very conversant with modern as well as antient literature, we cannot suppose them unacquainted with the plays of Cervantes, or of that voluminous author, distinguished by the glorious title of the *Spanish Shakspeare*, Lope de la Vega. That these celebrated twin-writers were very assiduous in the search of an extraordinary character can be proved, from their having read Paul Jovius de Piscibus Romanis, and taken the whole character of Lazarillo, the nice feeder, from that author; who has, in very classical Latin, given at large the

character

character of a parasite and smell-feast, who, in search of an umbrana, after many disappointments, sat down at table with a courtezan, to enjoy his beloved fish. If the reader should desire to come at this proof of their indefatigable diligence, without consulting P. Jovius de Piscibus Romanis, which is, I believe, not very common, he may turn to the article Chigi in Bayle's Dictionary.

The plays, said to be written by Lope de Vega, amount to the incredible number of 1800; all which were acted, and the greatest part of them with applause. Lope may be truly said, like Pope, to have *lisped in numbers*, for he began to make verses before he had learned to write. He bribed his elder schoolfellows, with a part of his breakfast, to commit to paper the verses he had conceived.

Before Shakspeare, as far as we can learn, began to write for the stage, Lope was a volunteer on-board the famous armada destined for the destruction of this country. And, not long before that pe-

 riod,

riod, as we are told by Cervantes himſelf, in his Prologo to his Comedias, the Spaniſh ſtage was in a wretched condition. Comedies were paſtoral dialogues, with interludes, in which the ribaldry of a black ſlave, the boaſting of a coward, and the blunders of a Biſcayner, reſembling our Teague's bulls, formed the principal part. To them, it is ſaid, we owe our Bobadil. All the apparatus of their theatre, ſays the ſame author, might be wrapped up in a bag; — being nothing more than four gilt leather ſkins, and as many falſe beards and heads of hair, with three or four ſticks, or ſheep-crooks. They had no changes of ſcenes; no paſſage for the actors in the center of the ſtage, the whole of which conſiſted of a few boards laid over benches. An old curtain, drawn acroſs, divided the part where the actors dreſſed; and the muſicians ſang without the aſſiſtance of inſtruments.

While the Spaniſh theatre laboured under theſe diſadvantages, a genius, who may

may be properly ſtyled the Spaniſh Roſcius, ſtarted up in the perſon of Lope de Rueda, whoſe dramatic pieces are ſtill extant, and confer honour on his memory. This man was a gold-beater by trade; and ſurely it is praiſe ſufficient for him to have Cervantes for his panegyriſt, who declares, that none ever equalled him as an actor, or in the natural turn of his dialogue and truth of character.

His prologues and interludes are diſtinguiſhed by the name of Paſſos, compoſitions at this day known by the name of Loas Entremeſes and Saenetes. Lope de Rueda died at Cordova, and, in conſideration of his great merit, was interred in the cathedral between the two choirs.

Noharro, a ſucceſſor of Rueda in acting, was an approved imitator of his maſter in the low comic. In his days the bag was withdrawn, and gave way to trunks, which held the ſtage-furniture.

Cervantes, ſoon after his redemption from ſlavery, in 1580, turned his ſtudies

to

to the theatre, and wrote *Los Tratos de Argel*, or The Humours of Algiers; and between twenty and thirty other comedies, which were acted, but never printed. —— The names of those plays, which were printed, are, *La grand Turquesca*, *La Batalla naval*, *La Jerusalem*, *La Amaranta o Mayo*, *El Bosque amoroso*, *La Arsinda*, and *La Confusa*. He was the first who divided the Spanish drama into three jornadas, or acts. He was likewise a strenuous defender of the antients, on which account he attacked his rival, Lope de Vega, with all his might; but the latter, by indulging the bent and humour of the people, and by being possessed of a rich and most exuberant fancy, with a just delineation of character, like the force of an impetuous torrent, bore down all before him. His invention was so fruitful, and his productions so rapid, that he did not give the public leisure to distinguish the efforts of genius from the wild sallies of intemperate fancy.

Calderone,

Calderone, who ſoon followed Lope de Vega, gave the finiſhing hand to the plan of his predeceſſor, and, with the ſame advantage of language and wit, debauched the taſte of the people. In the ſcenes of this writer, the fair ſex are taught to ſacrifice every thing to the impulſe of love, to deſpiſe the injunctions of parents, and yield to the arts of ſeduction. This author's wit is the more dangerous from being delivered in expreſſions the moſt captivating and beautiful. But this cannot be ſaid of all Calderone's plays; ſome of them I have read, which do not merit this ſevere cenſure.

Lope de Vega was ſo extraordinary a genius, that it is with difficulty we can quit a ſubject ſo agreeable. Some particulars of his life are ſingular and worth knowing.

When he was five years old, he could read Spaniſh and Latin, and make verſes with fluency. At the age of twelve, he was maſter of the Latin tongue and a com-

plete

plete rhetorician; he could then, too, dance and fence with eaſe and dexterity, and ſing in a tolerable taſte. At his firſt entrance into life, he became an orphan with every preſſure of diſtreſs. He was taken into the ſervice of the Biſhop of Aviler, in whoſe praiſe he wrote ſeveral paſtorals, and made his firſt dramatic eſſay, in a comedy called *La Paſtoral de Jacinto*. — Soon afterwards, we find him ſecretary to the famous Duke of Alva, whoſe praiſes he ſang in his Arcadia. About this time he married a lady of faſhion, on account of whoſe gallantries he fought a duel; and, having dangerouſly wounded his adverſary, he fled to Valencia, where he reſided ſeveral years. On his return to Madrid, he loſt his wife; and, being ſeized with the military ardour, he went on board the grand armada. In this expedition, ſo glorious to England and diſgraceful to Spain, De Vega loſt his brother, who was killed in a naval engagement. — Lope had his ſhare in the general misfortune

tune of his country, and appeared at Madrid without a ſingle friend. The Count de Lemos, ſenſible of his merit, made him his ſecretary. He now ventured upon a ſecond marriage with a woman of rank. This lady was Donna Juana de Guardia, whom he ſoon after loſt. Inconſolable with theſe afflictions, La Vega entered into the ſtate eccleſiaſtical, and was ordained a prieſt. He ſtill courted the muſes, as the chief relaxation of his ſorrows. He was now become ſo illuſtrious, that Pope Urban VIII. ſent him a degree of doctor in divinity, and the croſs of the order of Malta, added to a lucrative poſt in the apoſtolic chamber. This he enjoyed to his death, which happened in the ſeventy-third year of his age, to the great regret of the court and every learned man in the kingdom. — He was moſt magnificently interred at the expence of the Duke of Seſa, his patron and executor. The duke invited to the interment all the grandees of the kingdom. The funeral obſequies laſted three days; all

all the clergy of the king's chapel aſſiſted; three biſhops officiated pontifically; three eminent orators exerted themſelves in the praiſes of the deceaſed, with whom, when living, many princes gloried in being acquainted.

When Lope de Vega walked in the ſtreets of Madrid, he was gazed at and followed as a prodigy. He was loaded with preſents; by the rapid ſale of his works, he accumulated a capital of 150,000 ducats, beſides his annual income, of 1500 ducats, ariſing from his benefices and employments.

So great were the fertility of his genius, the readineſs of his wit, rapidity of his thought, and animated expreſſion, that there never was a poet in the world, either antient or modern, that could be compared to him. His lyric compoſitions and fugitive pieces, with his proſe-eſſays, form a collection of fifty volumes; beſides his dramatic works, in twenty-ſix volumes; excluſive of four hundred Autos ſacramentales, all which were ſucceſſively brought on the ſtage. What is ſtill more ſurpriſing, we have his own authority to ſay, that they formed the leaſt part of what ſtill remained in his cloſet. By exact computation, this author wrote twenty-one millions three hundred and ſixteen thouſand verſes. So extraordinary was the quickneſs of his fancy, he would finiſh a play in twenty-four hours; and ſome comedies he completed in leſs than four hours. It was not, ſays my author, his fault, that ſome of his immediate ſucceſſors had not his talents, and only imitated his imperfections; for the Spaniſh drama grew inſupportable when deprived of the beauties of Lope. This was foreſeen by Cervantes, who reproaches our poet with deſtroying the rules of the drama to court popular applauſe. And indeed Lope, in ſome verſes which he publiſhed, owns the charge; the purport of which is, 'That he was ſenſible of the reproaches, which the critics of Italy and France would make him, for breaking through all rules to pleaſe an ignorant public;

lic; but, ſince they paid for it, they had a right to be pleaſed in their own way.'

But that, which gives the greateſt luſtre to the name of De Vega, is derived from his perſonal virtues, which were ſuperior to his literary talents. His benevolence and charity towards the diſtreſſed were ſo great, that he ever extended his hand to the needy; inſomuch that, notwithſtanding his great wealth and large income, not more than ſix thouſand ducats were found in his poſſeſſion at his death.*

This much I thought was due to the memory of ſo great a genius, the contemporary of Shakſpeare, and ranked with him in fame.

I have owned my inability to trace Beaumont and Fletcher in the plots, characters,

* For the account of the Spaniſh theatre, and the life of Lope de Vega, I am obliged to my friend, Mr. Bowle, of Idmiſton; Mr. Hayley's copious notes to his Eſſay on epic Poetry; but more eſpecially to ſome valuable letters of an Engliſh Traveller in Spain, publiſhed by R. Baldwin, Pater-noſter Row.

racters, and situations, of the Spanish dramatists, though it can hardly be doubted, but that they would make use of that which they could so easily reach, and which they so well understood.

Of the fifty-four dramatic pieces, written by these great poets, two only at present preserve their rank on the stage, the Chances and Rule a Wife and have a Wife. No writers, sure, ever experienced such a reverse of fortune! To be tumbled from the highest exaltation of fame to neglect and oblivion is a mortifying lesson to all successful writers!

Mr. Garrick was often called upon, by the admirers of our old bards, and more particularly by Mr. Colman, in a letter, addressed to him, containing reflections on our old English dramatic writers, not to confine his labour of love to Shakspeare, but to extend his plan, and to open the rich treasures of Fletcher, Jonson, and Massinger; and more especially to take into his theatrical roll those admirable plays, the Maid's

 Tragedy,

Tragedy, King and no King, Philaſter, the Elder Brother, and the City Madam. Theſe, in the names of Burbage, Taylor, and Betterton, he conjured our great Roſcius, to reſtore to the public. And here, I doubt, ſomebody might hint, it were to be wiſhed that Mr. Colman had not employed the names of thoſe celebrated old comedians as a powerful charm to prevail on Mr. Garrick to grant his requeſt, who never wiſhed to hear the name of any actor but one.

But this excellent friend of the playhouſe and players, Mr. Colman, not content with inforcing his arguments to convince the manager of the great powers of writing which lay dormant in theſe dramatiſts, twenty years ſince revived Philaſter, with great ſucceſs, at Drury-lane, in which he introduced to the public a young and great acting genius, and gave an opportunity to the accompliſhed Mrs. Yates to diſplay her talents in a new walk of elegant ſimplicity. Bonduca he reſtored, with

with approved alterations and much applaufe, at his theatre in the Haymarket.

Unwearied in his affection to this *par nobile fratrum*, fome years fince Mr. Colman, undertook the publication of an edition of their works in ten volumes octavo. In this he has carefully fupplied the defects of former editions; nor has he omitted to do all poffible juftice to the commentators, Meffrs. Theobald, Seward, and Symfon, whofe merits he has candidly acknowledged, and has inferted all fuch notes of theirs as tend to illuftrate the text of the authors. And, what is much to his reputation, he has not, in his criticifms, indulged himfelf in the illiberal cuftom of infulting his predeceffors.

The comedians, too, are obliged to this writer, for refcuing *them* from the contempt and fcorn thrown upon them by feveral editors of Shakfpeare. In one part of his preface, he candidly acknowledges that the ftage owes its attraction to the actor as well as the author, with this happy illuſtration : ‘ For, if the able performer will not contribute to give a poliſh and brilliancy to the work, it will be, like the rough diamond, obſcured and diſregarded.’ In another part of it, he endeavours to heal the wounds made by the ſtings of the irritable Pope : ‘ Cibber, idle Cibber,’ ſays this agreeable author, ‘ wrote for the ſtáge with more ſucceſs than Pope. Æſchylus, Sophocles, Plautus, and Terence, were ſoldiers and freemen ; Shakſpeare and Moliere were actors.’

Mr. Colman perhaps had forgotten, that Æſchylus was a great actor as well as a renowned ſoldier ; that he not only acted the principal parts in his tragedies, but compoſed the muſic for them, ordered what particular dreſſes ſhould be worn, and projected all the machinery ; and, laſtly, that he diſtributed the parts, to the reſt of the players, ſo marked and noted that they could not poſſibly miſtake the proper pronunciation of every line. Sophocles underſtood the art of acting ; but the weakneſs nefs of his voice prevented him from joining the profeffion of player to that of author.

But, to return to Beaumont and Fletcher. After all which the warmeft admirers of thefe writers can fay in their commendation, the great preference, given by the public to Shakfpeare, may be eftablifhed on a lafting foundation, without in the leaft diminifhing their real and intrinfic merit.

I have ever looked on Beaumont and Fletcher as the difciples, or rather the dramatic offspring, of Shakfpeare; and fuch an offspring as will ever reflect great honour on the parent.

His firft uncontefted dramatic piece * is fixed, by Mr. Malone, to the year 1591, when Shakfpeare had arrived to the age of twenty-five. Fletcher was then in his 14th or 15th year, and Beaumont a child of fix years old. The earlieft of their productions cannot, I believe, be traced far-

* Love's Labour loft.

ther back than early in the reign of James I. —— Notwithſtanding what is ſaid by Seward of their predilection for Ben Jonſon, and Beaumont's imitation of his manner, in perſonifying paſſions rather than in drawing characters, I am perſuaded that they both chiefly formed themſelves on Shakſpeare, many of whoſe admired plays had been acted long before the fame of Jonſon was generally known. They, as well as the great poet, took their plots from hiſtory and romance. Their characters, like his, are as various as nature could produce, and, in moſt of their pieces, admirably and faithfully delineated; their ſentiments are tender, pathetic, and forcible, as plot, ſituation, and character, require. Their dialogue is univerſally allowed to be free, elegant, pleaſant, and witty; in general more adapted to the converſation of gentlemen than Shakſpeare's. And this excellence we may obviouſly conjecture to have proceeded from their higher rank in life and more poliſhed education; the ſons of a biſhop and a judge could command

mand a choicer ſet of companions than a poor player. But, though I grant their ſcenes abound more in liberal and high-ſeaſoned dialect than Shakſpeare's, yet, whenever he thinks proper to introduce wits, and treat his audience with gay converſe, he is not only equal, but ſuperior, to his imitators. For whom will they match with the ſprightly Mercutio or the humourous Benedic? To ſay nothing of the pleaſantries of the amiable Roſalind, what dialogue can be put in competition with the lively, witty, varied, mirth, the rapidly-facetious and laugh-winning repartees, of the Prince of Wales and Jack Falſtaff?

It muſt alſo be allowed, that the ſcenes of theſe twin poets are often blotted with unpardonable licentiouſneſs and ſtained with vile obſcenity. It is not enough to ſay, in their defence, that the poets of their age wrote in the ſame ſtyle. They have gone beyond all that I ever read of thoſe times in illiberal freedom. Seward, indeed, coldly owns, that Shakſpeare does not offend, in this point, ſo often as they do. But I will be bold to aſſert, that, compared with theſe authors, he is modeſt and chaſte, and writes like an anchoret. A diſpaſſionate and candid reader cannot help ſuggeſting, that the ſcenes of our great dramatiſt ſeem to have been acted before different auditors than thoſe of Beaumont and Fletcher. Innumerable inſtances of unlimited licenciouſneſs may be produced from many of their plays. I need only refer the reader to the Captain,—the Scornful Lady, ſince altered, much for the better, to the Capricious Lady, at the deſire, as I have heard, of an eminent actreſs, who performed the principal character,—and the Cuſtom of the Country. To this freedom of ſtyle they in ſome meaſure owed the ſucceſs of their dramas in the reign of Charles II. They approached nearer, in dialogue and character, to the colour of the times, than the plays of any other author.

But

But there is a wide difference, in the management of their plots, between Shakſpeare and Beaumont and Fletcher. Thoſe of the former are altogether as improbable as the latter. But, under his direction, improbability leſſens imperceptibly; the ſuperſtructure is ſo beautiful, that you forget the foundation. You ſurvey the whole building with ſuch delight, that you have not leiſure to think of the enchanted ground on which it ſtands.

Let me inſtance only the Merchant of Venice. Can any ſtory be deviſed more ſtrange and abſurd than a bond with a forfeiture of a pound of fleſh? But, when once you have admitted that into your belief, how does the poet, by the ſkilful texture of the ſcene, alarm your mind and work on your paſſions! Notwithſtanding the very odious character of the Jew, Shakſpeare has the art to intereſt you, for a time, in his favour. In the third act, we have a ſcene, reſtored to the ſtage by the ſuperior taſte of Charles Macklin, to

whom

whom indeed we owe the play as it now ſtands, in which the Jew's private calamities make ſome tender impreſſions on the audience; but the author, aware of the conſequence of indulging this pity, rouſes them to a juſt knowledge of his character, by making Shylock, in the midſt of his private addreſſes, give vent to his inveterate hatred to the Merchant, whoſe blood he determines to ſpill. The ſtory of the caſkets is as romantic as any tale of knight-errantry: in the hands of our enchanter it paſſes for true hiſtory. In the fourth act of the play, a young lady, in the dreſs of a lawyer, impoſes upon the high court of juſtice, and ſaves the life of the Merchant, by the help of a quibble: but the whole is conducted in ſuch a powerful manner as to juſtify the moſt diſcerning ſpectators in the approbation of the writer.

Let us now take a view of Fletcher's Wife for a Month, in which there are ſome juſtly-admired ſcenes, well-drawn characters, and much excellent ſatire.

There

There are, in this play, as well as in the Merchant of Venice, two plots: the putting up a lady by auction, as a wife for a month, and the recovering a ſick king by a doſe of poiſon.

Frederic, the King's brother, during the illneſs of the latter, takes upon him the government of the ſtate. His paſſions are vicious in the extreme: he plots the death of the King, and attempts the chaſtity of a noble and virtuous lady, the ſiſter of his miniſter, who, ſo far from endeavouring to curb his maſter's appetite, offers himſelf the willing pander in the management of the infamous buſineſs. Evanthe, the lady, is betrothed to Valerio, a young nobleman of great and amiable qualities.— Frederic conſents that the lover ſhall marry the lady, but under the injunction that he ſhall not cohabit with her more than a month. To complete the miſery of the unhappy pair, Sorano, the miniſter, ſuggeſts to his maſter the cruel plan of obliging Valerio not to enjoy his wife, under the

the forfeiture of her life. The ftruggles, arifing in the breaft of Valerio from this injunction, are well defcribed; an after-fcene, between the hufband and wife, terminates much to the honour of the lady. The King infults Valerio on his fituation, and receives from him fuch keen reproaches, as no tyrant, invefted with unlimited power, would tolerate. Evanthe difmiffes an attendant, who had always talked to her miftrefs in the language of the brothel, and had given her fuch advice as becomes the mouth only of a moft abandoned proftitute. A warm fcene enfues between Evanthe and the King, where noblenefs of fpirit is blended with vulgarity of language. Another interview follows, between the hufband and wife, where Evanthe is equally violent and fubmiffive. She is now put up to auction, the wife for a month. Three low wretches bid for her, but retreat as foon as they know the condition of marriage. Valerio, in difguife, with a forged ftory of his death, puts in his claim. As he he is going off with her, he is called back by the tyrant, who, on the appearance of Alphonſo, his elder brother, cured by the poiſon given by Sorano, is depoſed, and the lovers are made happy. Of Alphonſo's delirium, and the impropriety of amplifying in ſuch a ſituation, I have ſpoken at large towards the latter end of my remarks on King John. —— I need not ſay any thing of the conduct of this play, but the manners are ſtill worſe. That a young lady, in the pride of youth and bloom of beauty, ſuch as Evanthe, ſhould have warm deſires, when aſcending the nuptial bed, is what we expect; but ſurely modeſt reluctance in the lady will heighten her charms, and prove the beſt incentive to the lover. It is, in the language of Shakſpeare,

> ———— A pudency ſo roſy,
> As would warm old Saturn.

But Evanthe is ſo eager, that ſhe ſtimulates her huſband :

EVANTHE.

EVANTHE.

——— To bed, then:
——— Fie, my lord!
Will you put a maid to't to teach you what to do?
Are you ſo cold a lover?

Much more, and ſtill warmer, is urged by Evanthe; which is certainly extremely natural. But why not draw the curtains of the marriage-bed? Why will theſe writers, like Mrs. Behn, 'Fairly put all characters to bed, *and ſhew them there?*' However, this I ſhould have paſſed over, in our authors, as pardonable, from a young, exuberant, and vigorous, fancy, and ſuited to a tempting ſituation. But how the play of the Captain could be tolerated, by any ſpectators, it is impoſſible not to aſk.

Lelia, a lewd woman, tempts her own father, knowing him to be ſuch, to her bed. Struck with horror, he ſhudders at the thoughts of ſo ſhocking a crime. She perſiſts; and, by argument, ſtrives to reconcile him to the commiſſion of inceſt. —

This

This infamous woman, inſtead of being puniſhed, is married to a gentleman. It is inconceivable how any audience could ſupport ſcenes ſo unlike any of Shakſpeare, Ben Jonſon, and Maſſinger.

After all I have ſaid of the conduct and manners, in ſeveral plays, of theſe writers, I wiſh not to depreciate their real merits, or to blend their faults with their excellences. When their ſuperfluous and rotten branches are lopped away, there will be ſufficient remaining to flouriſh to all ages. I am firmly of opinion, that Beaumont and Fletcher are not ſo much excelled by their maſter's power of genius as his perfect ſkill in conducting his ſcenes to produce a happy effect. No man knew ſo thoroughly the meaſure of theatrical ground as himſelf. This ſeems to have been his great ſtudy.

Methinks I ſee him ſitting, unnoticed, amongſt the ſpectators, with deep attention obſerving the progreſs of the plot, the conſequence of character, the influence

of

of paſſion, the reſult of ſituation, and the general effect of the whole. No writer ever knew how to intereſt the minds of an audience, which is the great art of dramatic writing, like Shakſpeare.

Before I cloſe what I have to ſay concerning thoſe eminent writers, Beaumont and Fletcher, I cannot help obſerving, that the outcry, raiſed againſt thoſe ſpectators who did not reliſh the beauties of the Faithful Shepherdeſs, is not ſo well founded as is generally imagined. Ben Jonſon's cenſure is indeed almoſt ridiculous. How could he expect a mixed and rude audience, ſuch as that of London was in his time, compoſed of a few good judges and a rabble of ignorants, as he himſelf deſcribes them in his prologues and inductions, could taſte the beauties of ſo delicate and exquiſite a compoſition, which, for learned allegory, paſtoral manners, and variety and harmony of poetry, may challenge all that Greece or Italy, antient and modern, have produced? But it ought to be remembered, that, where characters are ſhewn on on the ſtage, of which the ſpectators have no reſemblances in their minds, it is impoſſible they can be intereſted for their fate.

Without conſiderable alterations, fine muſic, gay ſcenes, beautiful decorations, and excellent performers, I would not hazard the Faithful Shepherdeſs upon a London ſtage in theſe cultivated times. The univerſities of Oxford and Cambridge would, I believe, reflect honour on their own judgement by applauding ſo elegant a performance. It will give ſtrength to my argument, in favour of the ſuperior ſkill of Shakſpeare to govern the ſpirit of the public, to obſerve, that the paſtoral part of the Winter's Tale, Florizel and Perdita, without any aſſiſtance from the antients, or of modern Italy, perpetually triumphs over the paſſions of an Engliſh auditory.

I entirely agree, with the laſt editors of Beaumont and Fletcher, that Shakſpeare was not an aſſociate with Fletcher in wri-

 ting

ting the Two noble Kinſmen. The aſſertion, that it was ſo, is unſupported by any other evidence than the credit of a title-page. The publiſher knew very well, that, beſides the intrinſic merit of the piece, the names of Shakſpeare and Fletcher would operate as a ſuperior charm to vend the Two noble Kinſmen.

Beaumont and Fletcher ſeemed rather to have envied the ſuperior ſucceſs and merit of Shakſpeare than to have entertained any wiſh to cultivate his friendſhip. His name is mentioned in no poem of Beaumont; nor did Fletcher, though he ſurvived our great bard nine years, and the publication of his works, by Hemings and Condell, two years, join the chorus of the poets who ſacrificed to his manes.

This I do not give the reader as a certain proof that they were not acquainted, and did not live on friendly terms; but I ſee no reaſon to rob Beaumont and Fletcher of the honour of writing the Two noble Kinſmen, a piece which deſerves the beſt encomium

encomium the beſt writer can beſtow. But the ſtory of Palamon and Arcite is better adapted to that kind of poetry which the Italians call Romanza, and which celebrates acts of chivalry,—ſuch as Amadigi, Orlando innamorato, Orlando furioſo, and ſuch indeed as it was in the original of Chaucer, — than to a dramatic fable.

It has not been obſerved, I believe, that three queens ſupplicating, in this play, are borrowed from the chorus of Argive ladies in the Ικετιδες of Euripides.

Downs has placed Rule a Wife and have a Wife ſecond in ſucceſſion to the Humourous Lieutenant; with which play the king's company opened Drury-lane theatre, the 8th of April, 1663. It was performed twelve times ſucceſſively.

Hart and Mohun were much celebrated for their excellent action in this comedy: the latter in Leon, and the former in Michael Perez. Mrs. Marſhal, the greateſt tragic actreſs of that company, repreſented

 Margaretta;

Margaretta; and Mrs. Boutel, celebrated for the gentler parts in tragedy, ſuch as Aſpaſia in the Maid's Tragedy, Statira in Alexander, played Eſtifania with applauſe.

As I have not before me the novel of Cervantes, whence the plot of this comedy is taken, it is not in my power to ſay what particular uſe our authors made of their original. Whether we examine the main plot of the comedy, or the epiſodical part of it, we ſhall pronounce it a very entertaining and truly dramatic piece. The honeſt ſcheme of Leon, a man of honour and courage, to reſcue a fine woman, of large fortune, from her own perverſe will, from purſuing the gratification of inordinate appetite and paſſion, under the veil of a huſband whom ſhe purpoſed to make the blind for her pleaſures, is well conceived and artfully conducted. Michel Perez, the military coxcomb, who fancies himſelf ſuch an object of attraction, that every fine lady who views him muſt immediately fall

in

in love, is, by an artful intriguing girl, brought, by ludicrous contrivances, to a juſt ſenſe of his folly. Cacafogo was intended, as I have been told by the old actors, a rival to Falſtaff. If ſo, there never was ſo complete a triumph over impotent rivalſhip as that of Shakſpeare. Cacafogo reſembles the fat knight in nothing but cowardice. Though Falſtaff ran away as faſt as his legs could carry him, *when there was a hundred upon poor four*,* yet he was never ſo diſgraced as to take a kicking.

When Rule a Wife and have a Wife was repreſented, above half a century ſince, at Drury-lane, the elder Mills acted Leon, Wilks Perez, Mrs. Horton Margaretta, Eſtifania by Mrs. Oldfield. Booth certainly would have been an admirable Leon; for he had enough of comic humour for the aſſumed folly of the part,

 and

* Henry IV. Firſt Part, act II.

and abundance of manly fire and noble action to diſplay, when he broke through the cloud of his diſguiſe, and proved himſelf the vindicator of his own honour, and the worthy huſband of the lady he had married. But Booth avoided a contention with the impetuous Wilks, the avowed patron of Mills; he was beſides too indolent to ſtruggle for thoſe parts which apparently claimed his animated exertion.

The comic humour of Wilks was ſo intimately blended with the elegant manners of the gentleman, that his performance of this part, commonly called the Copper Captain, was eſteemed one of his beſt-repreſented characters. Mrs. Oldfield's Eſtifania was an excellent counterpart of comic ſpirit to the ſprightly humour of Wilks. When Ryan and Mrs. Younger, about the ſame time, acted theſe parts at the theatre of Lincoln's-inn Fields, it was univerſally allowed, that, though they were comedians of great merit, they fell infinitely ſhort of their competitors. ——

When

When Oldfield drew the piſtol from her pocket, pretending to ſhoot Perez, Wilks drew back as if greatly terrified, and, in a tremulous voice, uttered, *What! thy own huſband!* Oldfield replied, with an archneſs of countenance and half-ſhut eye, *Let mine own huſband, then, be in his own wits*, in a tone of voice ſo exactly in imitation of his, that the theatre was in a tumult of applauſe. Woodward and Mrs. Pritchard, Mr. King and Mrs. Abington, without having ſeen theſe great performers, have very happily diverted the audience in this and the other ſcenes of the play.

In the year 1759, Mr. Garrick revived this comedy. It was wiſhed, by Mr. Moſſop and his friends, that the two principal parts might have been divided between him and the manager; Moſſop Leon, and Perez Garrick; but Roſcius determined otherwiſe. Though he was an improper figure for the man whom a lady chooſes by her eye, he determined to act Leon, and give the other part to Woodward. Garrick, indeed, might plead, that Major Mohun was admired in Leon, though certainly not a perſon of large figure, as we underſtand by what Nat. Lee ſaid to him on his acting Mithridates: ‘ Thou little man of mettle! if I ſhould write a hundred plays, I would write a part for thy mouth.’

Mrs. Cibber inſiſted upon injuring her own conſequence, if that were poſſible, by acting Eſtifania. But Melpomene could not transfer herſelf into Thalia; after a few nights trial of her comic abilities, ſhe reſigned Eſtifania. It was then delivered to Mrs. Pritchard, who acted it with much applauſe.

Mrs. Clive had an undoubted claim to this part, as the ſuperior comic actreſs of the theatre. But neither maſter nor man, neither Garrick nor Woodward, wiſhed to ſee her in this play; and I firmly believe they kept her out of it from a tribute which they paid to her ſuperior abilities.

Though

Though Garrick's perſon did not preſent us with the true figure of Leon, and he was obliged to curtail ſeveral lines which deſcribed him as the author intended him to be in repreſentation, yet his performance was ſo much in truth and nature, that the ſpectators wanted neither height nor bulk. He wore the diſguiſe of folly, to intrap the cautious Margaretta, ſo exactly and humourouſly, that he preſented the complete picture of a Wittol. When he put on the man of courage, and aſſerted the honeſt rights of a huſband, no one of a more brawny or ſinewy figure could have manifeſted more fire or beautiful animation. The warmth of his ſpirit was ſo judiciouſly tempered, his action ſo correſpondent to his utterance, his whole deportment ſo ſignificant and important, that I think I never ſaw him more univerſally captivate the eyes and ears of an applauding theatre.

The players ſeem, in general, to confine the word *feeling* to the tender and pathetic parts of

tragedy.

tragedy. I ſhall beg leave to extend it to rage and horror, as well as grief and love, in tragedy; to the repreſentation of mirth, gaiety, pleaſantry, and humour, in comedy. I underſtand the rightly *feeling* a part to be the comedian's properly becoming, in voice, action, look, deportment, any attitude or ſituation of character whatever. When the Duke of Medina, in this play, ſaid to Leon, at the cloſe of that important ſcene in the third act,

I pray, ſir, uſe your wife well,—

thoſe, who remember Garrick in this ſituation, will recollect with pleaſure his moſt expreſſive look and action, when, ſheathing his ſword, he uttered this pertinent reply,

My own humanity will teach me this.

END OF VOL. II.

INDEX to VOL. II.

A.

B.

Buckingham

J.

K.

L.

Lope

M.

Massinger's

N.

Noharro,

R.

S.

Sejanus,

Swift,

Wilks,

END of INDEX to VOL. II.

ERRATA to VOL. II.

Page 172, line 6, For Johnſon, *read*, Jonſon.
—— 197, — 1, For Q. Ligarius, *read*, C. Ligarius.
—— 198, — 19, dele the word *for*.
—— 244, — 11, after the word *recitation*, add, *of ſentiment*.
—— 258, — 5, For Mrs. Boheme, *read*, Mrs. Seymour.
—— 364, — 16, for *grandmother*, read, *mother*.